The famous King Ranch brand being heated in the fire (above) and the legendary Peppy San Badger (Little Peppy) right.

The main entrance to King Ranch (shown above) and the main house at King Ranch (shown below).

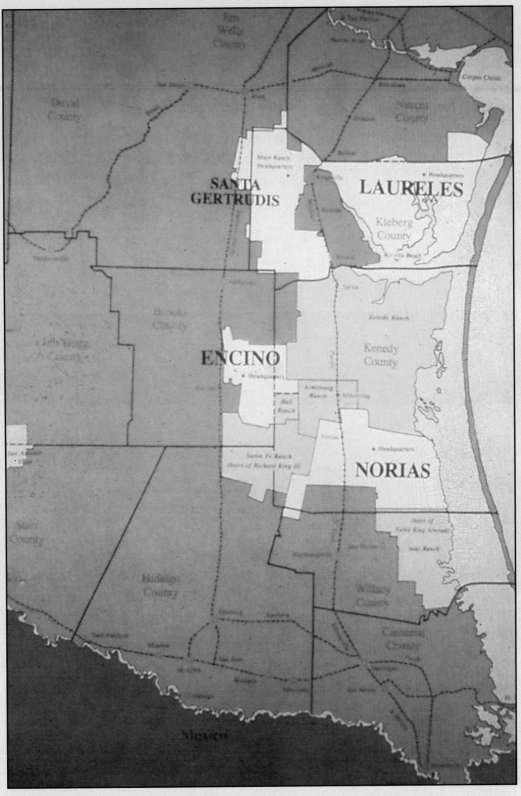

King Ranch, located at almost the end of Texas, in part where land joins the sea.
Its 825,000 sprawling acres give the King Ranch the reputation of being the largest
ranch in the nation. Shown above are the four subdivisions of the Ranch: Laureles,
Santa Gertrudis, Encino and Norias.

Peppy San Badger (Little Peppy), the legendary sire of King Ranch.

FORWARD

King Ranch has been a member of the American Quarter Horse Association since its formation and a continuous breeder of registered American Quarter Horses since Wimpy received AQHA's registration No. 1. To date, King Ranch has bred more than 6,600 foals which indicates the popularity of their bloodlines and the effectiveness of their breeding program.

Just as important, they have reached beyond the boundaries of North America to introduce the American Quarter Horse to Europe, Australia and South America.

In addition to breeding outstanding American Quarter horses, the Kleberg family has had a tremendous impact on the American Quarter horse Association through their insight and leadership.

Robert Kleberg, Jr., Richard Kleberg, Jr., and Tio Kleberg have been inducted into the American Quarter Horse Hall of Fame in honor of their involvement with the breed, as have two King Ranch American Quarter Horses: Wimpy and Old Sorrel.

This is quite an accomplishment for one ranch. The American Quarter Horse Association and the American Quarter Horse breed have been fortunate to have the King Ranch and Kleberg family actively involved for more than 50 years.

Bill Brewer
Executive Vice President
American Quarter Horse Association

DEDICATION

To Ronnie,
an amazing calm
amid the storms of life

Printed in the United States of America by
PrintComm, Inc.
1451 Empire Central, Suite 106
Dallas, Texas 75247
(214) 630-6601

ISBN 0-9649288-1-7

Typeset by Pro Publishing
Rte 2, Box 118
Boyd, Texas 76023
(817) 433-5232

Cover design by:
PrintComm, Inc.

Extra copies may be ordered from:
LMH Publishing Company
Route 2, Box 60
Groesbeck, Texas 76642
1-800-729-2234

Library of Congress Cat. Card No. 96-78900

TABLE OF CONTENTS

Acknowledgements

History plays an important role in all of our lives. It is a parent, guiding us in today's decisions; a teacher, steering us around the potholes of life, and a friend, wrapping us in warm memories. It is history that provides us with information on outstanding bloodlines of horses that lived before us; it is history that blesses us with the intrinsic wisdom of men who walked in an earlier time.

Unfortunately, by not recording today for those who follow tomorrow, we have lost much of the history of the western world. In its place the neon lights of Hollywood have written a sometimes tainted historical script for us. For that reason, I am deeply indebted to King Ranch for wisely preserving the story of King Ranch and Little Peppy. I am also deeply indebted to them for allowing me to be a part of that preservation.

I especially thank Helen Groves who had enough faith in my ability to write this book to suggest to King Ranch Board of Directors that I chronicle the history of Little Peppy. I owe thanks to Helen, to Tio and Janell, to all of the Ranch personnel who worked with me, including the researchers of King Ranch Archives - too many to name in fear that I might overlook someone - for their stories, the lifeblood of any good book.

As with all my work, completion would never be possible without assistance from many behind-the-scene folks: Myra Franklin, who edited the words in their infant stages; my mother Mondell Helms, who checked facts and read chapters; pedigree expert Larry Thornton, who patiently provided me with information and crash courses in equine genealogy, editor Glory Ann Kurtz who edited and typeset the final manuscript.

Lastly, I thank my family, who refuse to allow me the luxury of procrastination, and who always encourage my writing. A special thanks to my patient husband, Ronnie, who now expertly operates a washer and dryer and who knows our home-town fast-food waitresses on first-name basis. This book was born only because of all of you.

The Legacy to the Legend

Captain Richard King

Married

Henrietta Maria Morse Chamberlain

Alice Gertrudis King

Married

Robert Justus Kleberg, Sr.

Mamie Searcy

Married

R. M. Kleberg, Sr.

Sarah Spohn Kleberg

Robert Justus Kleberg, Jr.

Helen Mary Campbell

R. M. Kleberg, Jr. *(Dec.)*
Married
Mary Lewis Scott

Stephen "Tio" Kleberg
Married
Janell Gerald

Robert "Bobby" Shelton
(Dec.)

Helen King Kleberg Groves

Peppy San Badger
"Little Peppy"

		Leo
	Leo San	
		San Sue Darks
Mr San Peppy		
		Pep-Up
	Peppy Belle	
		Belle Burnett

PEPPY SAN BADGER
"Little Peppy"
1974 sorrel stallion

		Grey Badger II
	Grey Badger III	
		Mary Greenock (TB)
Sugar Badger		
		Lucky Jim
	Sugar Townley	
		R.J. Clark mare

BREEDER: R. H. Fulton And Co., Lubbock, Texas
OWNER: King Ranch, Inc., Kingsville, Texas

ACHIEVEMENTS

1977 NCHA Futurity Champion
1978 NCHA Derby Champion
1978 AQHA Register Of Merit
1980 NCHA Reserve World Champion
1980 Inducted into NCHA Hall Of Fame
1981 NCHA Open Finals Champion

THE
FOUNDATION

AN HONOR BESTOWED

*W**hile darkness struggled to maintain its reign over the early South Texas morn, warm glowing golds of the approaching sun quietly caressed the sky, loosening the night's hold and casting a kaleidoscope of colors on the horizon. Mornings can be exceptionally beautiful in South Texas. Steve Knudsen, an employee of King Ranch, knew that, and while climbing into his truck to head to work, he glanced toward the sky, reassured to see it was going to be a gorgeous day for the ceremony.*

Even though dawn was barely breaking, an early hour for a teenager, 14-year-old Amy Knudsen climbed in the truck to go to work with her father. Since it was summer vacation, she could have slept in for awhile, but not today; today was to be special and she wanted to be a part of the activities. Today, King Ranch was being honored by the American Quarter Horse Association and the excitement was contagious.

Upon reaching the Ranch, Steve headed straight for the stall of Mr San Peppy, the stallion better known in the performance world as "Peppy." On the other end of the barn lived "Little Peppy," the nickname for Peppy San Badger, a stallion also of celebrity status in the cutting horse world. The two renowned horses, playing an important role in King Ranch's recognition, needed to look their best today; it was Steve Knudsen's job to see that they did so.

Peppy, munching on his morning hay, looked up at Knudsen, unconcerned, as he unlatched the stall door. Although 28 years old and having been a workhorse all his life, he maintained the physique of a horse years younger. Those years of physical activity and his daily exercise program were still paying off with big dividends.

Even though Peppy was a stallion, Knudsen, who by now had spent almost 20 years with the old man, had no qualms about his young daughter being in the stall with them. Although cantankerous at times, Peppy was never offensive or destructive, even often seeming to prefer the company of children to that of adults.

Amy picked up a brush on the way to the stall, just like her father, and began attentively rubbing the stallion with long strokes. While she brushed on one side of him, Steve, noticing shavings in Peppy's foretop, reached up to knock them out. Peppy, however, immediately raised his head, just high enough so that the foretop could not be reached, while casting knowing eyes down at his caretaker.

Amy giggled, "He doesn't want you to do that, does he?"

"Naw," answered Steve, preferring to agree than to explain that Peppy knew at this moment he could be in control. Since he was in Peppy's stall and without a halter, Steve couldn't force the stallion to lower his head. Glancing at his daughter, he was about to instruct her to go for a halter, but abruptly changed his mind when he saw the look of bliss in her eyes as she affectionately brushed on Peppy. "Tell ya what," he said. "While you brush on him, I'm going to go down and check on Little Peppy. I'll get a halter while I'm gone so we can brush this ol' fella's foretop. Back in a minute."

Steve left his daughter and the stallion, both completely content with one another, and strolled to the other end of the barn to see Little Peppy. The stallion, hearing him approach, hung his head out the stall door for a moment of attention, an inquisitive, bright look shining from his keen eyes.

Little Peppy, a son of Mr San Peppy, was the winning hand Mr San Peppy had dealt to King Ranch. The stallion was a legend in his own time. Looking fit and feeling good, although no longer able to breed mares, it was sometimes hard to remember that Peppy San Badger was 22 years old himself. In his hey-day, he had not only won his share of championships, but later achieved the epitome of the King Ranch creed to sire offspring as good or better than the sire himself.

He had done that. His progeny of over 2,000 had put more stars in his crown than sand in an hour glass. With an affectionate rub on the stallion's head, Knudsen admitted to himself that Little Peppy deserved to have some years of retirement. Just as quickly, he admitted that today was not the time for reminiscing. The 2:00 p.m. ceremony would be here before he was ready if he didn't keep moving. Grabbing a halter, he walked briskly back to Peppy's stall; cleaning the stallion's foretop was his priority.

"Look Dad," stated Amy proudly, pointing to Peppy's forehead as Steve entered the stall. "Right after you left, Peppy put his head down and let me brush him off."

Steve Knudsen stared at the old stallion which slightly turned to look at him, eyes drooping sleepily while Amy continued to brush his forehead. The same horse, which had not allowed Steve to brush his forehead only minutes earlier, now stood, head lowered, his great power willingly relinquished to the innocence of the teenager.

By 1:30 p.m., the stallions, in full regalia, manned separate stations as their part of the dedication. While Mr San Peppy, with his 1976 World Championship saddle on his back, stayed at the King Ranch Visitor Center where the marker would be permanently displayed, Little Peppy stood guard at the entry of the Henrietta Memorial Center. Decked out in a prominent Running W saddle blanket, his 1977 NCHA Futurity saddle and a silver headstall, Little Peppy, the legend, watched as another honor was bestowed upon King Ranch, the legacy.

T oday, June 10, 1996, was their day. The American Quarter Horse Association was bestowing on King Ranch Historical Marker No. 11 for its indelible mark on the Quarter Horse industry, another milestone in the Ranch's illustrious career. The trustees of the program, which was administered through the American Quarter Horse Heritage Center and Museum, selected recipients who, through horses, people and events, made significant contribution to the American Quarter Horse history. King Ranch had blazed a trail in all

Bill Brewer from the AQHA and Tio Kleberg, King Ranch Vice President immediately after unveiling the AQHA Historical marker dedicated to the King Ranch. Photo courtesy of Hal Hawkins.

three areas and would, therefore, be awarded the prestigious marker.

THE PEOPLE

Achieving the award had begun over half a century earlier when, in the early 1900's, King Ranch heirs Richard Kleberg, Sr., Robert Kleberg Jr. and Caesar Kleberg brazenly experimented with a unique breeding program in search of a way to repeatedly produce superior ranch horses. Often they had found a horse with intelligence and cow sense, one which could handle the vast

Roberto Silguero (Beto) in his rain slicker begins moving the lead steers to start the work day. Photo by Janell Kleberg.

numbers of cattle daily worked on King Ranch, one with athletic ability to withstand the long, strenuous hours and with speed to corral wild strays who darted like mosquitoes from the herd. Yet, rarely were the animals able to pass these desired traits on to more than one generation of their offspring. King Ranch wanted a stallion which could sire as well, or better than himself, for generations to come.

For the Ranch, with its huge cattle operation, a breed of horses able to pass on its good genes was imperative. King Ranch men continually searched for the answer to this problem, passing on to their sons the unquenchable thirst for the superior sire, a pursuit of excellence that stood like an oath for each generation.

THE HORSES

The first inkling of success surfaced in 1916, when the "look,"as well as the bloodline, of a yearling grandson of Peter McCue and a son of Hickory Bill caught the eye of the Klebergs. This was approximately 20 years before the American Quarter Horse Association was even born.

Owned by George Clegg, a well-known Quarter Horse breeder, the colt was out of a mare with Thoroughbred blood brought to Texas from Kentucky. King Ranch purchased the yearling, named him Old Sorrel, and he spawned a kingdom of outstanding offspring, thus becoming the foundation of the famous King Ranch Quarter Horses. The forerunner of the historical marker presented to King Ranch by the American Quarter Horse Association was Old Sorrel.

When the American Quarter Horse Association was formed in 1940, its purpose was to perpetuate the Quarter Horse and thus produce the best type of riding horse available, including conformation, disposition and ability. The AQHA would then act as caretaker of the registration of these horses. To guarantee that only this kind of horse would be registered, a committee visited ranches who wished to register their horses, inspecting their broodmares. King Ranch passed the committee inspection with flying colors. In fact, according to an article by Hazel Bowman in the 1940 *The Cattleman* magazine,

Old Sorrel became the foundation sire of the King Ranch Quarter Horse Program. Photo by McGregor.

the committee regarded King Ranch stock "to be of such a high type that they will be beneficial to the breed." This, too, was the stock from Old Sorrel.

With hundreds of Quarter Horses to register, however, deciding who should get the coveted first number became quite a matter of discussion.

Finally, the founding fathers agreed that the horses should make the decision. Since the Fort Worth Fat Stock Show was one of the first shows of the year, the Grand Champion of that 1941 show would be recorded as the No. 1 horse in the registry of the American Quarter Horse Association.

King Ranch owned a stallion named Wimpy that Bob Kleberg knew could win the show. In fact, the year before, at the 1940 Fort Worth Fat Stock Show, another grandson, Peppy, who accompanied Santa Gertrudis show cattle to Fort Worth to display the benefits of King Ranch's line breeding in Quarter Horses, was entered in the Quarter Horse competition. Peppy won the blue ribbon as best Quarter Horse stallion of his class. He then returned to win the purple ribbon for Grand Champion of his class. Peppy was stock from Old Sorrel and Wimpy and was the same caliber of horse.

Wimpy earned the first registration number from AQHA by winning the Fort Worth Fat Stock show in 1941. Photo courtesy of J. A. Dodd.

Fort Worth was notorious for cold stock shows. With the unpredictable Texas weather, it could just as easily snow during the stock show as the sun could shine. The weather, however, was inconsequential to any good breeder in 1941. Anyone with a good stallion had intentions to be at the Fort Worth Fat Stock Show, rain, snow, or shine. Bob Kleberg was there with Wimpy.

When the dust settled after the 1941 Fort Worth Fat Stock Show, Wimpy was not only the blue ribbon winner of his class, but he also won the prestigious purple ribbon. He was Grand Champion of the show. His championship also won him the coveted first pedigree of the AQHA Registry. Wimpy was of the stock from Old Sorrel.

Mr San Peppy with mare manager Paul Studnicka and four Kinenos at the Visitor Center on King Ranch. The dedication marker in the background was presented by AQHA to King Ranch. (L to R) Studnicka, Jimmy Vela, Encarnacion Silva III (Chonito), Alfredo Mendietta (Chito) and Roberto Silva (Bobby). Photo courtesy of Hal Hawkins.

Some 30-odd years later, a stallion, Mr San Peppy, which sired another stallion, Peppy San Badger, was purchased by King Ranch. Their stories were almost "de ja vu" of Old Sorrel and Wimpy. While both stallions set world records, the Peppy San Badger lineage paid off in gold. Like Wimpy, Peppy San Badger became the new legacy of the legendary King Ranch, tying the past to the future. He, too, was of the stock of Old Sorrel.

Stallion manager, Steve Knudsen, carried Peppy San Badger "Little Peppy" to the dedication ceremony at the Henrietta Memorial Center. Photo by Janell Kleberg.

2

KING RANCH LIFE

*I*n 1969, Richard Nixon was elected President of the United States, remaining in office for the next 4 1/2 years and the Standard & Poor's index from January 1969 through January 1974 averaged +6.4 percent. Ray Price crooned to the Western world while World Champion cowboy Larry Mahan, fearless in his bull rides, kept rodeo spectators on their feet.

During the early 70's, the House and Senate wrangled over legislation to increase the pay for ranch and farm hands from $1.30 per hour to $1.70 per hour. In contrast, Texas & Southwestern Cattle Raisers Association President William C. Donnell testified in Washington that 450-pound steers of better quality in 1971 than those in 1951, sold for the exact same 40 cents per pound, although it was 20 years later.

And in the summer of 1971, Stephen J. Kleberg, nicknamed Tio, received his honorable discharge from the United States Army and was ready to go home.

Home was the fabled King Ranch.

Perhaps it was location, almost at the end of Texas, in part where land joins the sea, or perhaps it was its intimidating vastness, 825,000 sprawling acres, holding the reputation of being the largest ranch in the nation. For whatever reason, in the 1970's, when Tio Kleberg came home from the military, King Ranch remained a world of its own, a mystical oasis in a no-man's land of thorn bushes, wild animals, gopher holes, rattlesnakes and livestock. To the outside world, the Ranch, famous for its cattle and horses, as well as a regal beauty oddly born of desolation and allurement, had the ingredients of which dreams were made.

COMMUNITY LIVING

To those who lived there, it was a dream as well. Behind an unobtrusive entrance, King Ranch hummed with the business of living: sometimes the lulling drone of *siesta* time spent in respect for the heat of the day and sometimes the buzz of expediency when *vaqueros* rushed to beat the arrival of darkness. Besides the Main House and the homes of several descendants of Ranch founder Captain Richard King, a community of working people known as *los Kinenos*, meaning the people of King Ranch, also lived there. King Ranch fed them, cared for them and provided them with work, plenty of work.

The *Kinenos* had a colorful history of their own. "In the earlier years of King Ranch, Captain King went on a cattle-buying expedition to a drought-stricken ranching area in Northern Mexico," remembered Helen Groves, daughter of Bob Kleberg and a great granddaughter of the Captain. "Legend has it that he bought all of the cattle that had the '*viborita,*' the little snake brand, since it was hard for rustlers to change. After he bought the cattle, realizing there was nothing for the cowboys to do, and needing help himself, he invited them to come with him."

The people followed the Captain, bringing with them a vast array of knowledge about cattle and survival on land that often tested the tenacity of the toughest of them. Captain King's Ranch became their home and they became his people.

"Many of the *Kinenos* were born, raised and died right here on this ranch," explained fifth-generation descendent Tio Kleberg of the culture of a people who developed deep loyalty to King Ranch. "They take pride in

being the third-, fourth- or fifth-generation *Kinenos*. There's even an accredited school here that goes through eighth grade where the children receive a quality education."

The Klebergs and *Kinenos* have worked side by side for generations in the cow camps. Pictured at top are: (l to r) R. M. (Dick) Kleberg Jr., Lauro Cavazos Sr., R. J. (Bob) Kleberg Jr. and Helen C. Kleberg. *Kinenos* include (middle row, l to r) Jesus Muniz, Serafino (Pepino) Mendietta, Silvestre (Beto) Munoz, Pedro Olivarez, (front row) Francisco (Kiko) Gutierrez, Sixto Mendietta, Valentin Quintanilla, Pedro Trevino and Merced (Shorty) Muniz. Photo courtesy King Ranch Archives, King Ranch., Inc.

Besides the *Kinenos* and the heirs living on the Ranch, powerful people came and went. Just as they did in the early 30's, when Richard M. Kleberg Sr., Tio's grandfather and brother to Ranch master Bob Kleberg, held a seat for seven terms in the United States Congress, many a political heavyweight still put their feet under the King Ranch dining table. Past Governor John Connally, Governor Dolph Briscoe, Governor Bill Clements, Governor George W. Bush, as well as Presidents Nixon, Taft and Eisenhower considered King Ranch men their friends. Even prior to the formal meeting to organize the American Quarter Horse Association, an informal get together of interested parties gathered around the lunch table at Bob Kleberg's home.

It was easy for cattle to hide in thickets of mesquite on King Ranch. Photo courtesy King Ranch Archives, King Ranch, Inc.

Inside the prestigious homes of the caretakers, living seemed easy. The cool tile, the genteel courtly charm of its men, the polished silver and white-coated servants suggested a nobility of which cattle was king. With the coming of World War II, oil also flowed from beneath King Ranch soil, no matter if barren from drought or thickly carpeted with grass, and the wise investments from both paved the way for prosperous lifestyles and foreign expansion.

Outside the home, however, life was harsh. The constant battle to conquer mosquitoes and mesquite, to keep windmills turning and fences mended, built rugged men as tough as the boots they wore. In fact, it was the latter that allowed the luxury of the former. King Ranch, founded in 1853, and, therefore, a forerunner of Western ranching and customs, remained, even as late as the 1970's, a close replica to the tough individualism and romantic charm of the Old West.

ROUNDUPS, THE LIFEBLOOD OF KING RANCH

When Tio returned home, roundups, the semi-annual gathering of cow and calf from thousands of acres of brushy prairie, mirrored the very heart of King Ranch. Held in the summer months when children were out of school, roundups came alive with food, family and even fellowship, with outside visitors. During these times, the hierarchy of boss and cowboy was tossed aside while King Ranch heirs and *vaqueros* worked saddle-to-saddle. Ducking thorny limbs and splattering cacti, they adeptly collected cattle hiding in the thickets of mesquite, then conscientiously pursued the runaway strays in a fast trot, when possible, to protect their horses from mesquite stumps and gopher holes.

"It might take two weeks to gather all of the cattle, maybe 1,500 of them or more, since the larger pastures varied in size from 10,000-40,000 acres," explained Tio, today vice-president of King Ranch Inc. "All the cattle were gathered in a pasture, though, before we started working them."

Armed only with a string of horses, their favorite rope and an

The art of working cattle is a process learned over the years by the *Kinenos*. It is an art acquired as much by feel and experience as by knowledge and is engrained into them, beginning with their childhood years. Photo courtesy of Janell Kleberg.

innate knowledge born of the land, they gathered until every cow and calf was brought to the roundup. Herded tightly together, the bawling calves, their rusty brown hides wedged one against the other, resembled restless ocean waves, with their horns popping up now and then like white caps, as they hooked one another to obtain more room. There, on an open plain without modern-day stock pens, trucks or trailers, with the summertime 100-degree temperature even hotter from radiating heat of the packed bodies of hundreds of animals, they worked their trade.

Many a *vaquero* lived for the roundup, as did their sons who counted the days until school wound down and they could go "cowboy" with their fathers. At roundups, the little children decked out in straw hats of all sizes, importantly carried their own small rope, mingling among the working *vaqueros*, learning a future trade by watching, holding herd, roping "on foot" and being a part of a ritual as old as the Ranch itself. No one, yet everyone, cared for them.

"The kids learned early on to take care of themselves," recalled Leonard Stiles, at one time a special Texas Ranger with the Texas & Southwestern Cattle Raisers Association, who worked for King Ranch until his retirement. "They'd be out there when you're draggin' calves to the fire, right in the middle of it, trying to rope a calf's hind leg. A lot of times, they'd just be in the way, but that didn't matter. That was how they learned, and then they graduated up to really helping."

Tio began his roundup years as one of the young children patiently tolerated by a culture who believed in family values. Men, as well as women, kept children with them, the word "baby-sitter" non-existent in their vocabulary.

"The first time I remember Tio, he was probably 3 or 4 years old," stated Helen Groves, Tio's cousin and 20 years his senior. "We were at roundup and he was sitting on the back of a wagon. One of the favorite meals of the cowboys was mountain oysters, so they had a bucket on the back of the wagon where they tossed them after castrating the calves. That day, Tio stood there playing in the bucket, blood up to his elbows and grinning from ear to ear."

King Ranch, especially at roundups, spared nothing of the down-to-earth reality of life from its children. To be a part of roundups meant experiencing thorns, falls, kicks, blood and growing tough. "It was very family-oriented," acknowledged Kleberg. "Little kids, older kids, all ages were there. Those old enough to help did the running. They'd go get syringes, medicine, run the paint bucket or run the brand."

"Roundups were almost like a family reunion," added Groves, recalling that vastness of King Ranch meant workers could go all year without seeing one another. "Everybody was there or at least came by. We worked, but that was the fun of it."

Work began at the light of day, with horses already saddled by feel more than by sight, while darkness still engulfed the camp. Daily, they repeated the same ritual. In the morning, the cattle were sorted amid a constant cloud of dust boiling upward from restless hooves. Culling cattle too old to produce calves and gathering them to the side, the older *vaqueros* and younger boys held them in a herd of their own, while uneasy cows, bellowing for their calves, were held separately.

To the side of this organized chaos, out of the way of the cattle and cowboys, the cook parked his wagon, hoisting a long tent under which wooden tables stretched row after row. In the days prior to oil and roads, mules pulled the wagon to the site. By the 70's, however, the chuck wagon had undergone renovation.

Reynaldo De Luna (Sarco) is saddlin' up at the break of day at Norias remuda. Photo courtesy of Janell Kleberg.

"The wagon had rubber wheels on it and we'd pull it behind a pickup to camp," continued Leonard Stiles. "In there would be pots, pans, plates, skillets, groceries; everything a cook would need to fix a meal."

The sides of the chuck wagon, when folded up and fastened, except for its rubber wheels, made the wagon look like any other chuck wagon that might have traveled with the Charles Goodnight cattle drives years earlier. At cow camp, however, the sides unfolded, displaying shiny stainless steel unknown to the chuck wagons of the Charles Goodnight era. The stainless steel sides doubled as the preparation area for the roundup chef.

Lunch, served only after all of the sorting was done, mixed an uncanny harmony of sounds and smells. The aroma of mesquite-broiled meat hovered over pungent odors of sweat and leather, while bawling calves periodically drowned out the prattle of mealtime conversation.

While a few men held the roundup, the remainder washed up with whatever water was available. They then filed past the chuck wagon, filling their plates with beef and beans. Afterwards, climbing over benches, they plopped the heavily laden plates on the wooden tables, manners left back at the house, hungrily attacking the meal. As soon as some had eaten, they relieved those holding the herd. Besides refueling their bodies, lunch also gained them a momentary respite from the torrid sun. Work shut down after lunch with the number of calves to be worked that afternoon dictating the length of the break. It was this time that allowed the

A windmill pipe stretched between two mesquite trees made a saddle rack for cow camp. Photo courtesy of Janell Kleberg.

scorching sun to meander on across the sky while cowboys hunkered down under any available shade, waiting for the hottest time of day to pass, some quietly talking, some using saddles and chaps to caress their heads for a moment's rest.

"The windmill crew and the fence crew would show up to eat at cow camp as well, and later, when everyone reassembled for work, these men became the ground crew, building the fires and keeping them burning," explained Kleberg. "From then on, the work was like an assembly line for branding and castrating calves. As soon as one calf was done and turned loose, another one was there to be branded."

"Things had to move right along because all those calves had to be done before we lost daylight," added Helen. "Many times, there were as many as three to five men, all dragging calves to the fire at once, while those on foot 'mugged' them or heeled them."

Even with its sweat, grime and fatigue, the roundup sometimes turned into somewhat of a social event with people bouncing in their vehicles miles across the rugged land to dine at rough-hewn tables under the cow camp tents. The visitor might be a dignitary or a sister or brother. For a short while, they became a part of a passing era, witnessing work that tied man to the harsh land and livestock.

Water on King Ranch, generated by windmills is stored in huge, round troughs for the cattle. Photo courtesy King Ranch Archives, King Ranch, Inc.

By end of the long day, with branding and castrating finished, the cattle were sprayed, then held a while longer to allow cow and calf to "mother-up." Finally, they were left to drift at will toward the windmill and water while the men broke camp, preparing to proceed to another pasture at dawn. Tomorrow the ritual would repeat itself once more.

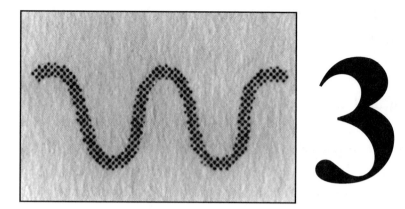

THE MEN AND THE MARES

*J*uly 1971. Tio Kleberg shoved the gear shift of his Opal Cadet station wagon into park, slowly turned off the ignition and gazed at the rambling home of his great Uncle Bob. Six months earlier, when Christmas lights twinkled throughout the town, he had sat in that same place, anxiety penetrating him then just as it did now.

Bob Kleberg did that to him. Talking with his great uncle always mingled fear with respect and sometimes even exasperation in him. Taking a deep breath, he reminded himself it was that way for everyone on the Ranch; Kleberg's presence had a way of demanding it.

Fresh from two years in the United States Army, following his graduation from Texas Tech University, Tio had come home to go to work, although at the moment he hadn't been hired. While there at Christmas, he approached his father, Dick Kleberg Jr., also a Ranch boss, about a job on the family Ranch once his military career ended. Sitting in the kitchen that day, Dick Kleberg's piercing blue eyes bore into his son and he quietly deferred that decision to Tio's Uncle Bob.

He said, "I can't hire you, Tio. If you want a job on King Ranch, you'll have to go talk to Uncle Bob."

Tio had not expected that answer but before the apprehension of speaking to his great-uncle about something other than every day matters overwhelmed him, he immediately left his parents' home, drove to Bob Kleberg's home and asked him for a job. It hadn't taken long. The elder Kleberg, a man known for rapid-fire decisions, whether at home or horseback in the pasture, answered quickly and to the point, "Come see me when you get out of the military."

And so he was here.

And, it was time to get on with it. Quickly, he grasped the door handle of the station wagon, thrust it open, and stepped into the July sun; the stark, South Texas heat a familiar greeting. Strolling briskly to the house, he found Bob Kleberg seated on the porch in his favorite chair, absorbed in the materials in his lap. After the normal greetings between the two men, Tio got right to the point. "I'm back, Uncle Bob, and I'm ready to go to work."

The master of King Ranch eyed his nephew momentarily. Then, without any suggestion of prior knowledge of Tio's arrival home, but with an authority that instructed and dismissed at the same time, he gruffly declared, "Okay, Tio. Then go report to your father."

"Yes sir!" answered Tio, relieved to be both formally employed and assigned to his father. It was good to be back on King Ranch; this is what he wanted to do and the years at college plus those in the military had given him time to realize that. Although he had known he would be hired after their conversation at Christmas, having to have another business meeting with Uncle Bob as a hopeful employee had just made him apprehensive.

Whirling into his father's driveway, he threw the Opal Cadet into park, and without hesitation this time, jumped from the car and bounded into the house in search of his father. "Dad, Uncle Bob gave me a job," announced Tio the moment he saw him.

"He did, did he? What did he tell you?" asked Dick Kleberg, the strong angular features of his face giving no hint that he already knew the answer.

"He said to come see you," answered Tio, relaxing in a chair across from his father.

The elder Kleberg said nothing, but picked up a Ranch gate key lying in front of him and handed it to his son. He then reached for a set of car keys, also lying close by, and tossed them to Tio as well.

"What are these for?"

"How in the hell do you think you are going to get around? There's a green Chevrolet Bellaire sedan in the front driveway. Those keys are for that car."

Seeing an ever-so-slight grin creep across his father's face, it dawned on Tio that the two older Klebergs had orchestrated today's "job interview." Before he could protest, Dick Kleberg motioned him toward the door. "Quit sitting around here; get to work, Tio."

Bob Kleberg Jr., the grandson of Captain Richard King and the elder heir to the Captain's dynasty, controlled King Ranch. His presence revealed a dominant, driving force of strength and leadership, causing Ranch employees to often enter his company with hat-in-hand, referring to him as "*el Patron*," the boss.

Even so, with the *Kinenos*, Kleberg managed to walk a tightrope of both boss and friend, listening to their problems and offering counsel to them on subjects they discussed with no one else. Though he was "*el Patron*," he was still one of them. A story from John Cypher's book, "*Bob Kleberg and the King Ranch: a Worldwide Sea of Grass*," paints an extraordinary picture of Kleberg.

> "A woman visitor approached an old man who was puttering around near the headquarters. She opened a conversation by asking him if he worked there; he acknowledged that he did.
>
> 'Then you must work for my friend Bob Kleberg!'
>
> 'No, Senora, I work for King Ranch. Mr. Kleberg, he work for King Ranch too.' "

"He was the boss," described Tio, "and he was tough as hell. I remember his favorite saying was 'no excuses.' Still, he was a very honest man and his word was the rule, so when he said something, you never had to go back. If he said 'yes,' that was it, and if he said 'no,' that was it."

Just like Tio, Bob Kleberg's daughter, Helen, remembered the strong character of her father. "Being one who loved to work, he expected everyone else to do the same," stated Helen. "He spent little time in the office and when he did, it didn't put him in a very good mood; he preferred to be outside physically doing things. He always said, 'I can make more money for this Ranch on a horse working in the roundup than sitting in an office.' "

In contrast to Bob Kleberg, slimmer-built Dick Kleberg Jr., the father of Tio and 18 years younger than his Uncle Bob, commandeered a quieter, second-in-command presence.

"Dad managed the horses and the cattle on the *Laureles* and *Santa Gertrudis* Ranches of King Ranch while Uncle Bob oversaw the two southern Ranches, *Norias* and *Encino*," recalled Tio.

In addition to his Texas work, Bob Kleberg also extended King Ranch to several other continents. Although he and his nephew shouldered responsibility equally, Dick Kleberg adhered to King Ranch protocol of respect for one's elders, acknowledging like the Ranch employees, the leadership of his uncle.

R. M. (Dick) Kleberg, Jr. Photo courtesy King Ranch Archives, King Ranch, Inc.

Bobby Shelton, a cousin to Tio, also worked on King Ranch, having returned there in the early 1960s. Shelton and his brother B.K. Johnson, whose mother, Sarah, was Bob Kleberg's sister, were orphaned at a young age and then reared by their Uncle Bob and Aunt Helen.

These were the men that Tio, christened Stephen J. Kleberg, joined in Ranch management in the summer of 1971. All were descendants of Captain Richard King and his wife, Henrietta. All were powerful men with strong wills and work ethics, motivated by the same goal of working the land to preserve, and thus improve King Ranch.

RANCH EDUCATION

Bob Kleberg was sometimes called "*el Tio*," meaning "the uncle" by some of the *Vaqueros*. As a child, Stephen Kleberg reminded them of his Uncle Bob and, therefore, he inherited the nickname "Tio." After the younger Kleberg grew past childhood play, he worked on all four of the divisions which comprised the 825,000-acre King Ranch. Most of that time, however, was spent on *Laureles* and *Santa Gertrudis* Divisions, the domains of his father.

"When I came back to the Ranch I was young, naive and eager to make my mark," remembered Tio. "Dad, in his wisdom, first assigned me to work for Emmert Crocker, the foreman of *Santa Gertrudis*."

Brothers Bob Kleberg Jr. and Dick Kleberg, Sr., were sons of Alice and Robert Justus Kleberg and grandsons of Henrietta and Captain Richard King. Courtesy of King Ranch Archives, King Ranch, Inc..

Crocker's Ranch headquarters churned with activity long before the sun rose each morning as the cow boss, the windmill crew and the fence crew gathered for an early morning cup of coffee and received their orders for the day. By daylight, the crews dispersed to fix broken windmills, mend fences and move cattle.

Crocker immediately enrolled the young Kleberg in some postgraduate Ranch education. When fences needed building, Tio accompanied the crew; at roundup time, he became one of the hands. When windmills croaked to a stop, he acquired the art of repairing them. For almost two years, he moved from job to job, mastering the skills necessary to get the job done, learning from the masters how to do it correctly. At the same time, each Ranch foreman under whom Tio worked instilled in him, as they had instilled in Shelton before him, the unwritten law of the land: to take care of those whose loyalty lay to the Ranch, while expecting a good day's work in return.

While the *Kinenos* taught Ranch basics to each younger generation, it was the heirs of King Ranch who passed on to them an intrinsic knowledge of good horseflesh. In order to harvest a quality foal crop each year, they used expertise in pairing mares and stallions that was not written in any text book; instead, the knowledge was gleaned year after year from practical application, where prairies and brush land served as classroom and teacher.

HORSES: THE HUB OF WORK

In the 70's, horses thrived on King Ranch, a major tool necessary for Ranch chores. Not just any horse would do in the sometimes hostile climate of South Texas, however, so King Ranch developed their own breed of broodmares, approximately 300 strong, in an effort to keep their cowboys well mounted. At that time, the working horses were kept in a *remuda* which was driven horseback for miles from one working place to another.

"The cowboys could do phenomenal things with their ropes but they had to have horses that allowed them to use them," remembered Noe Silva, at one time, a second-generation cowboy on King Ranch. "Ropes were weapons as well as tools, like an extension of their arm, and without a good horse that would let them   use the rope, they couldn't get their job done. The training these cowboys put on their horses in order to do their job is an example of how King Ranch had bred intellect into the animals."

23

In addition to good-minded horses that allowed cowboys to rope off their backs, King Ranch equines also showed instinct in holding cattle, separating calves from cows and tracking wayward strays.

"You'd better be hanging on if you heard the noise of a wild cow scratching against the brush," smiled Silva, commenting with the voice of experience. "Those horses would fly through that mesquite after the cattle and you had to be cowboy enough to ride 'em. The land was rough and the mesquite limbs could be like a

Bobby Shelton rides among King Ranch cattle. Photo courtesy of King Ranch Archives, King Ranch, Inc..

maze you're flyin' through. One horse couldn't handle an entire day's work like that so every vaquero had several horses he used to get the work done. I might have 10 head on my string while my dad always had 15 or more."

Just as Bob Kleberg cared for his employees, he also stressed care for the Ranch horses. The care of Ranch horses, however, differed from the care of performance horses like cow chips differ from gold dust. Ranch horses in hot, dusty pastures miles away from a barn, without water hoses or horse brushes, received little of the bathing and brushing that performance horses received. Still, the range's code of horse care, no matter how primitive, carried honor, and, therefore, reflected a *vaquero's* horsemanship.

If water stood in the trough when a *vaquero* brought a tired horse to the *remuda* to exchange for a fresh one, range-land etiquette demanded he toss a bucket of water on the horse's back. Then, picking up a crusty, dry, cow chip from the dirt, he used it as a brush to rough the wet hair.

"Even if there wasn't any water, you at least roughed the hair where the saddle was," commented Helen. "Anyone who didn't do that was not considered a good horseman.

"Their feet were also tended to when they started getting long to keep them from splitting," she continued. "They trimmed them by using a sharpened crowbar and a hammer; the two objects together were almost like toenail clippers. They would pick one foot up gently with a rope so the horse wouldn't jump around and, if necessary, they'd use a twitch on him. Although most of the horses never wore shoes, they all got their feet trimmed."

MARE SELECTION

Just as well-oiled machinery improves production, the Kleberg men continually experimented with their equine breeding program, trying to improve the quality of horseflesh, their machinery that directly affected Ranch work. The process involved the selection and grading of mares and colts and it cycled throughout the year.

"We'd round up approximately 300 mares that roamed the brush land just like the cattle," remembered Tio. "It usually took about 10 days riding from sunup to sundown to gather them, since they ran in large pastures when not with the stud."

During his first year back at King Ranch, Tio rode with his father and Bobby Shelton to gather, appraise and cull the mares, learning that which he had witnessed as a youth but now from the perspective of a man. Dick Kleberg's eyes, windows to a mind crowded with horse knowledge, became the texts that taught his son.

Those mares whose conformation excelled, whose appearance after a year on the range showed survival with little care, and whose disposition reflected good minds, earned "staying rights" at the Ranch. They were then assigned according to their strengths and weaknesses to a stallion whose genes would hopefully help develop the strengths and overcome the weaknesses. The goal was a superior foal, both physically and mentally.

Months later, the process repeated itself; this time, though, to sort the new foals by the mares' sides. Once again, the men spent long, hot days riding among inquisitive colts, looking for the soft eye that meant a good mind, the long hip and good straight legs that meant athletic ability.

"After the foals were weaned," continued Tio, "we graded them again, that second time separating approximately 25 of the best ones for the annual King Ranch Yearling Sale."

Unlike many ranches that only used geldings, King Ranch adhered to a different standard, using its mares prior to sending them to its broodmare bands.

"I remember how it was when I first came here and witnessed the process of what you might call 'natural selection' of horses based on

A *vaquero* and his rope were the lifeblood of the King Ranch. Photo by Janell Kleberg.

performance," recalled Tio's wife, Janell. "The cowboys rode everything: mares, geldings, stallions. They were all working horses. A cowboy kept a string of horses of various talents and seasoning: a stout horse that could crack brush all day long on the hottest day in August; a strong, fast horse for roping and a quick horse for weaning calves, each with good sense, personable nature and sound."

Using mares in roundups had a two-fold purpose. Besides an animal to use for working, it also allowed viewing a future broodmare in action, experiencing her disposition; seeing whether she had the strength for dragging calves and the fortitude to accept the long hours of hard work. The best mares were easily spotted but, rather than leave them on the job, they were graduated to the broodmare bands, hopefully to pass on their good minds, their cow sense and physical ability to their foals.

"Although each spring, the *vaqueros* were asked to put their best mares in the broodmare band," added Janell, "in return, when the colts were ready to break, the cowboy was given first choice of the colt his mare foaled."

The foal to the *vaquero* was like a grandchild to a grandparent. He often experienced traits and quirks he had known in the mare and enjoyed experiencing the fulfillment of another generation to maturity. However, the young foals were not rushed into the working world.

"The mares were at least 3-years-old before they were sparingly used on roundups, since these younger ones weren't strong enough for the work, yet," explained Helen. "For a long time, the 2-year-olds, and those just turned 3, were mainly ridden by the kids to school.

"Mares who couldn't produce these kind of foals, those which weren't good in ranch work or who weren't easy keepers, were culled," she continued. "In a terrible drought, the mares had nose bags and were fed oats, but if there wasn't a drought, then they had to be able to live on the land."

Years earlier, in cattle experimentation, Bob Kleberg had begun a program of line breeding through which was created a new breed of cattle, the Santa Gertrudis. Since the program had worked well with cattle, Kleberg, whose analytical mind constantly pursued the challenge of reproduction, introduced line breeding into the Ranch horse program.

For years it worked well. The quality of the broodmare bands excelled as the mares fulfilled their part of King Ranch objective: to harvest a foal each year as good as, or better than, its parentage. With time, though, the upward spiral of continued improvement slowed, a byproduct of the genetic similarity between the stallions and the mares.

"The key to the success of line breeding over a long period of time is the infusion of strategic out cross blood," stated pedigree expert and author Larry Thornton. "The out cross blood is needed to help prevent the undesirable side effects of inbreeding. Although King Ranch insured an out cross blood in its line breeding program, by using stallions without King Ranch breeding to sire its broodmares, over the years the mares became genetically similar, homozygous in much of their genetic makeup. At the same time, the stallions were genetically similar so that pairing the two didn't get enough genetic diversity to continue improving the foals. They needed a new out cross to give it a genetic boost."

That out cross was later to come in Peppy San Badger. At that time, however, the answer to the problem had yet to appear.

"I asked my Dad one evening, 'How do you produce better stallions?' " remembered Tio. "With the number of mares the Ranch was breeding, I could not understand why we were not producing better babies."

Years of breeding had taught the elder Kleberg, however, that patience and time solved many problems. He was relying on that lesson to return the spark to their Quarter Horse program. Once healthy and fit, without an ounce of fat on his trim body, emphysema had begun to take its physical toll on Dick Kleberg, thus quenching some of the old flame that had once fervently burned in him to sustain the reputation of King Ranch horses.

Most likely he recognized in his son flickering images of himself years earlier. Steeped, though, with the line breeding tradition, he answered what he truly believed. "It takes time, Tio. It just takes time and breeding."

LOOKING AT NEW BLOOD

The sun peeked over the horizon as Dick Kleberg, dressed in his King Ranch uniform of khaki shirt and pants, pants legs tucked into his boot tops, strolled toward his Buick, a hat pulled low to shield his eyes from the sun's brilliant orange glow. No oxygen today, he thought, pleased to defy the tank that controlled many of his days. Yesterday's rain, settling the dirt and clearing the air, made it easier to breathe.

Although his usual high level of energy had faded with the progression of his emphysema, and although now days he rarely ventured from the house without his oxygen, this day was different. He felt better this morning than he had in a while, and he had plans for it.

Thinking about his plans, he slammed his hand into his pants pocket and fumbled with the small white box he had gotten from a dresser drawer only minutes earlier, reassuring himself that it was still there. Lincoln Borglum, the renowned artist whose father, Gutzon Borglum, had sculpted Mount Rushmore, had given him a *gold medallion as a gift years ago. On one side was the famed King Ranch bull, Pepino, and on the other, the famed King Ranch horse, El Nino. In addition, Borglum had placed an inscription around its border which read, "Presented to RMK and MLK."

Kleberg was so impressed with the gift that he later had several more made. They were his gifts to people who earned a special place in his heart, his way of *telling them so. His sons and daughter had one. Today, he planned to give another.*

Smiling to himself as he cranked the car, he threw it abruptly into reverse and backed out onto the road. He knew Leonard Stiles was wondering what was the matter with him. Leonard had been his right-hand man for years. Before leaving the house, he had called Leonard on his radio and gruffly told him to meet him at the "Muerto" pens. The word meant "dead" in Spanish.

The pens were quiet, no cattle, no cowboys, no work, as Kleberg sat gazing at the area waiting on Stiles. In only a short time, he saw his Ranch manager drive in behind him, get out of his truck and start walking toward the car. Kleberg loved to pull pranks, but this wasn't a prank and he felt himself getting emotional. To buy an extra moment for composure, he pretended not to see Stiles' arrival, and slowly moved the car forward, gaining speed as Stiles began trotting.

Stiles, realizing his boss was up to something, immediately returned to his truck, jumped in it and floor-boarded the accelerator, quickly overtaking Kleberg's Buick. Veering the truck off of the beaten path into the stubby grasses, he passed his boss, then swerved the truck in front of him, forcing Kleberg to stop.

Intrigued by the antics, Stiles jumped from the truck and strode to the driver's side of the car. That was the customary place for employees to stand when talking to the boss. Kleberg, once again in control of himself, acted as if it was the first time he had seen Stiles.

"Get in! get in!" ordered Kleberg, motioning to the passenger side of the car.

The instructions took Stiles by surprise, and he hesitated for a moment before circling the Buick. Ranch etiquette dictated that cowboys didn't get in the car with the boss. Something really was up. Apprehensively, he walked around the car. As soon as he had settled himself in the seat, Kleberg picked up a small box and handed it to Stiles.

"Here, I want to give you something," said Kleberg.

"Naw, don't do that," began Leonard, but Kleberg quickly interrupted him.

"Yeah, take it, take it."

Stiles, who had been on the receiving end of many of Kleberg's jokes, gingerly took the box, held it away from him and slightly pointed it toward Kleberg so that anything that might jump, pop or spring from the box, would do so in his

30

direction. Slowly he lifted the top. There on a bed of white cotton lay a gold medallion.

"Leonard, keep that in your pocket and you'll never be broke," stated Kleberg, cranking the car at the same time, a sign of dismissal for the Ranch manager.

Strengths, when taken to extremes, become weaknesses. Yet, rarely does that happen overnight. Neither had it been that way with the offspring born among the sage and prairie grass of King Ranch. Just as breeding for excellence came slowly, losing that edge evolved slowly as well. The first hint of the declining bloodline happened when one year, the new crop of colts, which frolicked and played in the thousand-acre pastures, were only graded "good." The next year, the grade was the same, as was the year after that.

"Good," however, was not superior and, therefore, not acceptable when a 100-year-old reputation for "breeding the best" was at stake. No one liked sliding from first place, especially Tio, and the failing quality of King Ranch foals gnawed at his gut.

What bothered him even more was that Ranch interest in the famed King Ranch Quarter Horse program seemed to be declining as well, as if something was sucking the lifeblood from both the breeding program and the foals' quality. With his father's health failing and Uncle Bob neck-deep in the management of ranches on other continents as well as at home, he chose to pursue the puzzle alone, at least at first. The bloodline for superior horses was there, though; visible, and maybe not too late to do something about it.

Silently, Tio wondered if the problem might lie with their stallions. For years, genetics dominated dinner table small-talk as well as conversations in the pastures. He felt strongly that was where the problem began, otherwise, the decline would not be so uniform. What might happen, he wondered, if King Ranch mares were crossed with other stallions, stallions not belonging to King Ranch? What if new bloodlines were brought in, rather than only using their line-bred stallions?

In some ways, it felt like he was committing treason to think opposite of his father; to wonder if line breeding, the star of the King Ranch's Santa Gertrudis program, might be stunting the equine program.

Tio was not alone, however, in his progressive thinking. Another young cowboy, Joe Stiles, had joined King Ranch as Ranch manager of the horse operation the same year Tio had retired from the service. Joe's dad, Leonard Stiles, managed cattle on King Ranch. Having spent several years on the rodeo circuit, Joe, familiar with several bloodlines, spent hours telling Tio stories of other horses he learned about, while Tio was polishing his army boots. The two speculated what might happen if the strong, well-minded King Ranch mares, with their excellent conformation, were bred to aggressive, outside stallions.

Through trial and error, Tio learned breeding for excellence was more than the science of mating a good mare and a good stallion. Photo courtesy King Ranch Archives, King Ranch, Inc.

The seeds planted in the young ranchers' minds sprouted an itching desire to 'look around' at available horses, and the best display of horseflesh: the Ohio Quarter Horse Association's All-American Quarter Horse Congress in Columbus, Ohio, was in progress. As home for two weeks to some of the best-bred horses in the nation, the show generated a breeding ground of information, a place where interested horsemen could not only learn about stallions but see their offspring perform as well.

King Ranch had exhibited horses in AQHA shows in the 50's and had kept ties with the American Quarter Horse Association. While the sun still warmed the earth in South Texas one October morning, Tio and Joe boarded the King Ranch plane, stepping from it long hours later into the nippy fall air of Columbus, Ohio.

"We just went up there to see what was out there. We wanted to know what other people were doing and where we might go with the mares," remembered Stiles. "Although King Ranch had a tremendous herd of mares, the emphasis had been taken from the breeding program for a while, and we wanted to renew it."

The All-American Quarter Horse Congress teemed with activity. Barn after barn held stalls and make-shift stalls to house the large number of exhibiting

King Ranch fillies. Photo courtesy of Janell Kleberg.

horses. Kleberg and Stiles wandered up and down the alleyways, peering into the stalls to view horses from "the outside world" and studying the pedigrees owners proudly taped to the stall doors. For days they warmed the bleacher seats in the show building, watching all types of horses, that sported no King Ranch blood, perform in classes such as Western pleasure, roping, English, and reining. Continuously, one of the men extended an arm and finger, pointing out to the other, those horses that struck their fancy. Congress was like an ice-cream store; it had every flavor of horse anyone could desire.

Everywhere they went - while standing in line for a cup of coffee, chatting with exhibitors bathing a horse, sitting next to a stranger in the bleachers - they talked with stallion owners. Some, like used car salesmen, wore big smiles, slapped them on the back and bragged about the qualities of their stallions back home. The conversations, somehow, left Tio with a queasy feeling.

Time and again, they slowly strolled the red carpet of the prestigious Stallion Alley, where, unlike the used car salesmen, owners exhibited their high-dollar stallions in designer stalls, wooing the breeding public with photographs and success stories. A contagious, carnival-style excitement permeated the air, complete with cotton candy and hot dogs, and the two young ranchers caught new-stallion fever.

Kleberg especially liked the stallion, Impressive, which stood on Stallion Alley. He continually returned to the stallion's stall, moving slowly from one vantage point to another, viewing the bright young horse, whose body displayed power from all angles.

"He was such a good-looking horse," admitted Tio. "I remember telling Joe, 'That's it! That's the look we're wanting.' This guy had a tremendous hind leg."

As the two continued their search, Stiles met several old acquaintances from his rodeo days, many of whom, like Morgan Freeman of Skiatook, Oklahoma, owner of the well-known stallion Blondy's Dude, discussed performance horses, the kind that appealed to the men. Since Freeman annually came to the Columbus show, he had already learned that a golf cart was the best way to save boot leather while traveling the vast acreage of show grounds and shared the ride with the men.

Although the soil on King Ranch got hard, it in no way compared to the asphalt and concrete of the fairgrounds. Besides, on King Ranch, your feet usually hit the stirrups rather than pavement. Gratefully, Kleberg and Stiles rested their aching feet in Freeman's golf cart, at times enduring race-car-style driving as Freeman, quite experienced in golf cart maneuvers, swerved in and out among people, horses and dogs, carrying them from show arena to show arena. Always, they discussed horses, questioning Freeman about bloodlines; in turn, he showered them with information about Blondy's Dude.

"We especially liked the colts of Two Eyed Jack, a stallion owned by Howard Pitzer; Double L Straw, a stallion owned by Coffey Jameson Quarter Horses, and, of course, Blondy's Dude," noted Kleberg.

Back at King Ranch, the trip to Congress occupied most of Kleberg's waking hours, having only increased his appetite to consider other stallions in King Ranch's breeding program. Conversations between him and Joe always turned to bloodlines and pedigrees they witnessed there. Still, for the three stallions they preferred, Two Eyed Jack, Double L Straw and Blondy's Dude, it had been their offspring, and not the stallions themselves they had seen. Therefore, they decided the best thing to do was go see them.

"When we actually saw Two Eyed Jack, Double L Straw, and Blondy's Dude, all three were really what we anticipated them to be," stated Stiles. "I remember Double L Straw was leggier, more a running-type horse than I thought he would be, but we liked all three of them."

While the stallions in "vogue" to the outside breeding public ignited new foal ideas in Tio, he had yet to share any of his thoughts with his father. Confident, though, that new blood would improve the quality of King Ranch Quarter Horse foals, he decided to discuss his ideas with Dick Kleberg. Although he expected his father to agree, he wanted the right opportunity, a time when it was just the two of them and they had plenty of time to talk.

"I approached Dad about the subject one morning while we were horseback, grading colts for the upcoming King Ranch Sale. There was this scrawny, big-headed colt out there and I made some brash statement about how we could do better than that."

35

Dick Kleberg realized there was more to the statement than just words from an obstinate young man. Pulling on the reins, he stopped his sorting and rested both hands on the saddle horn. Expressionless, he listened while Tio told the story of visiting the stallions. He shared his dream of a new breeding program and the mixing of the foundation King Ranch blood with new blood. Tio stressed that by breeding now, next spring they would most certainly have an outstanding young colt on the ground who would then mature into an elite breeding stallion, the kind that would assist their excellent bands of broodmares to once again produce foals of outstanding quality.

King Ranch broodmares. Photo courtesy King Ranch Archives, King Ranch, Inc.

He had never considered that Dick Kleberg would not accept the idea. It seemed so simple and necessary; he felt sure his father would see that if you took good mares to a good stallion, you would get good babies. How hard could that be?

The elder Kleberg had been aware of the jaunts his son and the Ranch manager had taken looking at horse flesh so the subject was not unexpected. What was unexpected to Tio, however, was Dick Kleberg's answer. He remembered well the conversation with his father that followed his unfolding of a new breeding plan.

"He listened to me and then he let the air out of my sails," admitted Tio. He said, 'It won't work. The odds of sending a mare off and raising a stud colt that is good enough to come back into your broodmare band is one in 10,000. Trying to find a good stud is hard; trying to raise one is harder and raising a damned good one is near impossible!' "

After Dick's knifing answer, silence injected a widening gulf between the two of them. Dick stared at the colts grazing in front of them. Perhaps it was the memory of his own young manhood and the dreams that had then flooded his mind; perhaps he liked the grit his son had shown by checking out horses and presenting his idea. For whatever reason, while his mind assured him the program would not work, his heart encouraged him to let experience be a teacher for the younger man.

Leonard Stiles and Mac Wood of Briggs Ranch. Leonard was the recipient of the bronze medallion from Dick Kleberg, Jr. Photo courtesy King Ranch Archives, King Ranch, Inc..

"Then he told me," continued Tio, 'If you want to do it, though, you can try it.' "

Tio grabbed the ray of light Dick Kleberg extended; it was all he needed to pursue the new breeding program. Within a few days, several hauling vans pulled away from King Ranch loaded with 20 mares for each stallion. Blondy's Dude, Double L Straw, and Two Eyed Jack, headed for new courts, new blood and the beginning of a journey for a new stallion, leaving behind a long-standing tradition of keeping King Ranch propagation within its fences.

The following year, as the yellows and pinks of the wild flowers announced the birth of spring, new foals with fresh blood frolicked the grassy plains of King Ranch. The experimental breeding program continued for several years, allowing the first foals to mature, thus unfolding the nucleus of a probationary program.

"Dad was right. We produced some nice colts," acknowledged Tio, "But we didn't get the stallion I wanted. Neither was I aware of some of the problems we'd get when we carried our horses off. We took mares that had never been off King Ranch and, therefore, had lived in a closed environment, out into a new environment. We exposed them to sicknesses and accidents that we didn't normally have on the Ranch and, naturally, they brought these problems back with them.

"Then, there was the cost of transportation for that many mares plus the cost of breeding fees and board. For such a large number, it proved to be unprofitable year after year."

While the offspring were good, as the elder Kleberg had predicted, there was no great, young prospect with the regal look of a King to become heir to a band of King Ranch broodmares. Tio, however, still believed in his idea. He adamantly wanted to somehow improve the quality of King Ranch stallions but began to ponder the wisdom of his father's words.

Maybe his father was right. Maybe he couldn't improve the quality of foals by sending that many mares out in hopes of getting a good stallion.

Maybe the stallion who would be "the King" of King Ranch Quarter Horses had to be purchased, not raised.

*Editor's Note: Today, Leonard Stiles, treasuring his gift from Dick Kleberg, keeps it on him at all times. It is carried inside his billfold, first placed in a plastic cover, then wrapped in a sheet of paper on which is written, "Presented to RMK and MLK; Medal Lic. Art Co; N.Y. Bronze. Medallion presented to Leonard Stiles by Dick Kleberg."

THE VIGOR OF CUTTING BLOOD

"*W*elcome ladies and gentlemen to the 1973 National Cutting Horse Association 11th annual Futurity! The cattle are now settled and we are ready to get under way with this year's Finals.*"

With that announcement, Helen Groves turned her attention away from her father seated next to her and back to the Fort Worth Will Rogers Coliseum arena where the cattle stood quietly, eyeing the horses walking toward them. Settling back into her seat, the anticipation buoyed her excitement which had been slowly growing this week over her horse, Pay Twentyone. Tonight he was showing in the Futurity finals.

For just a moment, she reflected on the last few fast-paced days. Last night was the semifinals performance and afterwards out to eat. Then, this afternoon, she and her trainer, Red Stephenson, had gone out to a ranch for Red to tune the horse, after which she hurried back to attend a Calcutta held earlier this evening. Now...

Suddenly, the crowd roared with the quick moves of the first horse working, bringing Helen back from her thoughts. The sights and sounds were addicting. All of a sudden, her pulse raced with the propelling movements of the horse. There was just something about this cutting...

"I really liked cutting when I got into it," stated Groves reflecting on her introduction to the art of working cattle as a sport. As a young girl, Helen had literally helped separate thousands of calves from the herd during King Ranch roundups, but that kind of cutting was different. While it could sometimes get the adrenaline flowing, roundup on the Ranch was a mixture of work and fun, with plenty of "overs" should the calf escape. In the arena, though, you lose the calf, you lose the game, both with yourself and with others; no "overs" were allowed. Since she had a competitive spirit, she liked the sport.

In her youth Helen, had enjoyed riding and the roundups. There she had felt like a part of useful work while learning at the same time. At home there was no television to watch and the radio, which was for adult use only, came with a hands-off policy for her. That left her sitting on the huge porch or riding horseback. The two were like comparing apples to oranges; they had nothing in common. The porch offered much less freedom, especially when her father, in confidential conversations with *Kinenos*, gave her the same ultimatum for the porch as for the radio.

As Helen grew older, she traded roundups and King Ranch for marriage and Pennsylvania. Without wide open prairies in which to ride, she fox hunted, a sport she had started in boarding school in Virginia, as well as participated in other fashionable equine activities of that area.

"My mother told me about fox hunting when I was little," reminisced Groves of the memories shared with her by her Eastern-reared mother. "Her stories were always so vivid, and it sounded like such fun, so I started at Foxcroft Boarding School in Virginia and continued fox hunting at Vassar. Over the years, I played polo and I worked the ponies. My first husband and I ran a pony club for six years while our children were in it, and we went to the races a lot. The children showed and hunted in the fall and there were a lot of 23-hour days with horses; fox hunting at daylight, cattle work, pony club, racing and polo under lights."

Ironically, fox hunting opened the door for Helen's cutting interest. In the heat of the hunt, her spine, already weakened from other horse activities, absorbed jolt after jolt as the horse pummeled over obstacles and pounded down its course. At first, numbness took over her fingers, then pain, more severe with each ride, made standing straight, much less sitting in a saddle, unbearable. In search of a cure she visited doctor after doctor until an osteopath offered relief, finally standing her straight again. He admonished the young horsewoman, divorced by then, to never again ride horses or ride in jeeps, or to sit in cars or airplanes for more than an hour.

Since she was strong willed, like the King Ranch men, her love for horses overrode his admonitions. After several months of feeling fit, she donned her fox hunting paraphernalia to try the sport once again. It only took one hunt, however, to sideline her where the osteopath could not. Dejectedly, Helen tried to ward off a creeping, foreboding thought that she might never ride again, turning her interests instead, to settling in a new ranch in Middlebrook, Virginia.

One day, while working around the barn as her new employee, Harry Price, exercised horses, Helen shared with him her physical problems when she was horseback and her fear of never riding again.

"Harry suggested I might enjoy cutting," said Helen. "He had a flat saddle, more like those everyone rides today. I tried it and found that I could ride that."

Helenita Kleberg Alexander Groves (on horse), along with her mother, Helen Campbell Kleberg (Mrs. Robert J. Kleberg, Jr.) Photo courtesy King Ranch Archives, King Ranch, Inc.

41

Promptly, Helen traded in her fox hunting for a new sport on a flat-seat Western saddle. The next step was to find a suitable horse.

"I remember going to Polly Hollar's once to look at horses," smiled Helen ruefully. "I saw a Hollywood mare cut that I'll never forget. There are only a few runs that stick in your mind, but that was one of them."

Unable to find the right horse to buy before an upcoming cutting horse show in Great Falls, Virginia, Helen, determined to try her hand at competitive cutting, checked the rules of the National Cutting Horse Association, the governing body of the sport, and found that she could borrow a horse and show.

"In 1972, the rules were different from today," she explained. "As long as no money changed hands, someone could lend you a horse to cut on. You could pay the entry fee and keep the money, or the person who owned the horse could pay the entry fee and keep any money you won. I borrowed a horse, marked a 72, which was the high score for the day, and thought 'There's nothing to this.' Little did I know!"

With a winning run under her belt and her back accommodating the saddle again, Helen began purchasing fillies. Later, she traded two fillies for Harry Price's young stallion, Pay Twentyone, and then hired trainer Red Stephenson as her ranch trainer to ready the young stallion for the prestigious NCHA Futurity held in Fort Worth, Texas.

"The horse was already started when I got him," stated Stephenson. "He was real green but he'd had some cow work on him, and then I put about 11 months on him. At times he could be kind of studdy, but he was sure a nice pony."

Helen knew just the remedy for that problem. "He was so studdy as an early 3-year-old," she allowed. "But, we turned him out with some bred mares and they made a perfect gentleman out of him."

In the span of a year, fox hunting, polo and pony clubs joined yesterday's memories while the work of her youth, now took precedence as a sport. Helen was enjoying cutting horses and the foreboding thought of never riding again transcended itself into a memory.

In early December 1973 in Fort Worth, Texas, Pay Twentyone, scoring well in the two go-rounds and semifinals, qualified for the NCHA Futurity finals. Bob Kleberg flew in to watch his daughter's stallion perform. For Helen, it was a special treat to have her father attend the finals since he usually centered any frivolities around his King Ranch business schedule. In addition, he preferred Thoroughbreds and racing as his equine sport. Still, Bob Kleberg was a man known for his respect of a good performance horse and he had come for that reason. And because Helen was his daughter.

"I knew he would enjoy it because he loved a good horse," stated Groves, whose mother had died in 1963. "I didn't, know, however, that he had been to Fort Worth to a cutting before. In those days, we had a party for the owners and riders before the finals where people had a drink or two and participated in a Calcutta. While we were enjoying the party, he told me he attended a cutting in Fort Worth at North Side years earlier. He reminisced that though the spectators had been mostly ranch people, everyone dressed in black ties or gowns, as was the custom of the times, at Madison Square Garden Horse Show dressed for the evening. Daddy also remembered Burke Burnett standing up during the cutting and shouting at his rider to take the bridle off and let the horse work. He did and the horse won the show by cutting bridle less."

Kleberg wore a business suit to the NCHA Futurity finals. The *Patron* of King Ranch did not wear boots all of the time, sometimes leaving them and the khaki work clothes of the ranch at home. After the Calcutta, the father and daughter moved to the west side of the coliseum to box seats that trainer Red Stephenson had procured for them to watch the cutting from. Always one who came prepared to play the perfect host, Kleberg shared a drink from his flask with new found friends.

"As we watched the horses work and discussed them, Daddy thumbed through the Futurity program which listed all of the horses that had entered the Futurity as well as their dams and sires. He kept saying, 'Almost all of these horses go back to King Ranch stock. This horse goes back to this King Ranch horse and that horse goes back to another one.' "

Even Helen's stallion, Pay Twentyone, sired by El Pachuco Wimpy and out of Chiquita Veinte, was an example of King Ranch blood pouring through the veins of Futurity finalists. In the early 70's, however, Doc Bar blood was the up-and-coming bloodline to own in the cutting industry, dominating the primary breeding of many of the colts in Fort Worth. Doc Bar had sired the 1970 and 1971 Futurity Champions, Doc O'Lena and Dry Doc, thus sending the cutting horse community into a frenzy for Doc Bar blood. In fact, at the 1973 Futurity, Nu Bar, another son of Doc Bar was favored to win the Futurity. Still, the foundation blood of King Ranch Quarter Horses lay hidden in the background of many of those horses as well.

Stephenson and Pay Twentyone scored 214 in the finals to earn 9th place. "I probably beat myself in the finals," stated Stephenson, as he talked about Pay Twentyone's finals run. "The horse was kind of squeally, and so to combat that, I went out to Lynn Strickland's place and worked him and I had him too tired in the finals. I got my first cow set up pretty good and he was sharp, but he didn't have the quickness he

Bob Kleberg and his daughter Helen Groves. Photo courtesy of King Ranch Archives, King Ranch, Inc.

44

normally had. My second cow was one that wanted to run, but he stopped her in the middle of the pen. He missed her one time, but he recovered real good. I think if I'd had a little more spark, a little more animation, we could have been in the top three. We couldn't have won it, but we could have been up there."

Just making the finals on her first trip to Fort Worth was an impressive feat. The horses there also impressed Bob Kleberg.

"My father went home from the '73 Futurity determined that King Ranch would enter horses in the cutting arena," recalled Helen. "He asked Tio and Bobby Shelton to find the best trainer for King Ranch cutting horses and start the program."

In fact, at that very show, Tio and Joe Stiles sat high in the seats on the other side of the coliseum, having come to look at cutting horses for a Ranch sire. Kleberg was especially infatuated with Futurity finalist, Chunky's Monkey, ridden by Matlock Rose and owned by Douglas Lake Cattle Company. Interestingly, Chunky's Monkey's pedigree showed King Ranch blood since he was by Peppy San and out of Stardust Desire.

Pay Twentyone ridden by Guy Nelson. Photo courtesy Quarter Horse News..

"I remember the Futurity because of Matlock," smiled Tio. "I was just a kid when Loyd Jenkins showed horses for King Ranch but I remembered hearing names like George Tyler and Matlock Rose. At the time of the Futurity, we also owned half interest in Dash for Cash with B. F. Phillips. B. F., who was also involved with cutting, had been down at the Ranch and conversations inevitably turned to cutting.

"We went to the Futurity to check out the other options," he continued, "and set our sights for the horse program by seeing the Futurity and watching such outstanding athletes perform. We knew if we could get horses like that to breed on our mares, which were already selected because of their ability to work cattle, we might have something special."

In addition to Tio's interest, with Bob Kleberg showing a growing interest in cutting horses and with Helen Kleberg Groves already owning them, King Ranch was on the verge of making history again, this time with cutting horses.

The "sea of cattle" for which King Ranch became famous. Photo courtesy King Ranch Archives, King Ranch, Inc.

STEPPING STONES TO THE KING

MR SAN PEPPY AND MR. WELCH

A bout the time Tio Kleberg and Joe Stiles visited the All-American Quarter Horse Congress, searching for new blood to add to the King Ranch stallion battery, Buster Welch, a West Texas rancher, competed in cutting competitions across Texas, racking up one win after another. The horse he showed, Mr San Peppy, was continuing to carve on his reputation as one of the top cutting horse trainers in the industry. Mr San Peppy, a young stallion sired by Leo San, was out of Peppy Belle, a mare that happened to be saturated with King Ranch bloodlines.

Welch stacked up cutting awards like Babe Ruth hit home runs. He earned the NCHA World Championship in 1954 and 1956 on Marion's Girl, a mare owned by Marion Flynt of Midland, Texas. Marion's Girl, like the young stallion he rode almost 20 years later, had King Ranch blood in her veins, also. In addition to these two championships, Welch made the Top 10 in the cutting world six additional times.

Welch had also won the 1962 inaugural NCHA Futurity aboard Money's Glo,

*owned by C. E. Boyd of Sweetwater, Texas, and returned to win the second
Futurity in 1963 aboard Chickasha Glo, also owned by Boyd. Then in 1966,
riding Rey Jay's Pete, owned by Kenneth Peters of Fort Wayne, Indiana, he
captured his third Futurity title.*

*Five years later, in December 1971, about the time that Tio Kleberg had
questioned the continuing quality of King Ranch Quarter Horses, Welch won his
fourth Futurity on Dry Doc, a stallion owned by Chartier, Ward and Pettipren.*

*At the time of that championship, Welch already had Mr San Peppy, then a
3-year-old stallion in training, owned by G. B. Howell, from Sunland Park, New
Mexico. Mr San Peppy's bloodline traced back to King Ranch breeding and
would, therefore, join the growing chain of King Ranch bloodlines, like Rey Jay's
Pete and Marion's Girl, on which Welch had success.*

*Unknown at the time, he was also carrying the genes of the future King Ranch
legend.*

Charlie Ward, a California trainer, trailered Dry Doc, a young stallion
sired by Doc Bar, out to Buster Welch's ranch at Sweetwater, Texas,
in early January 1971. The young stallion, out of the great mare
Poco Lena and a full brother to the 1970 NCHA Futurity champion, Doc
O'Lena, was already well broke and ready to be started on cattle.

Welch received another 3-year-old, Mr San Peppy, to his barn four
months later. In contrast, Mr San Peppy was barely broke and, therefore,
late in the running for the upcoming NCHA Futurity that would be held in
December. It didn't take long for the trainer to know that talent oozed from
Mr San Peppy, but his confidence grew slowly in orchestrating that talent,
since the two racked up some harrowing experiences in their early days.

BREAKING MR SAN PEPPY

Race horse trainer Bubba Cascio approached Welch about riding the
young stallion. Howell had sent Mr San Peppy, along with his

Thoroughbred race prospects, to Cascio at the racetrack in El Paso for breaking, but Mr San Peppy did not take too well to racehorse jockeys. Quickly realizing the young Quarter Horse was the black sheep at the tracks, Cascio called Welch and asked him to ride the stallion, acknowledging, however, that he had bucked off most of the jockeys who tried to ride him. Since Mr San Peppy was a full brother to the good horse, Peppy San, Cascio felt it was worth the effort to break him. Welch agreed.

"Bubba thought he was a real good horse and wanted to show him, so at that time, it sounded like I would ride him three or four months and then Bubba would have time to fool with him," recalled Welch.

"A good jockey that worked for Bubba brought him over and he kept staying and staying, wantin' to see me ride that sucker since he'd bucked off so many of those race horse jockeys. I just stayed busy. But, the minute he left, I got on him, real easy-like and kept nursin' him around until I got him uncocked. After he was goin' good, I gave him to Rod Edwards who worked for me and told Rod to go climb mountains with him. I had everybody climbing mountains with him for a long time. Those mountains are good horse-breakers.

"One day, after we had him goin' pretty good, I let my mind wander off some place," continued Welch, "and all of a sudden, he bowed up with me and I knew immediately he was comin' out buckin'. Before I thought, I reached up and stabbed him in the shoulder with my spur, and boy, then he did do some buckin!

"He bucked all around that pen and finally into the iron fence, hit his head and fell on the ground. When he did, I went to workin' on him in the belly, but he was kind of on my foot, so I couldn't do a lot to him. When he came up out of that wreck, though, he never tried to buck again."

Then looking up over his glasses with a grin, Buster added, "Course, he had me bucked off when he hit that fence; he just didn't know it."

The bucking episode made a trainable horse out of Mr. San Peppy in a hurry, and although he still required extensive riding, the focus for Buster changed from concern about breaking a bad habit to concern about controlling a good one.

"He was a big-moving horse, a wild-moving thing," continued Buster. He had so much talent, it was mainly a matter of trying to get him to control those moves. He could run wide open and stop on a dime, but everything he did was violent; he didn't do anything easy."

Since Welch had Dry Doc primed and ready for the NCHA Futurity that December, he put young Greg, his son,

Buster Welch riding Marion's Girl for Marion Flynt. Photo courtesy of Buster and Sheila Welch.

on Mr San Peppy. The two did well in the first go-round, but Mr San Peppy's sweeping movements scattered cattle their second time out, eliminating them from the Futurity. Buster, however, on the back of Dry Doc, made history by winning his fourth championship at the NCHA Futurity.

THE MAKING OF MR SAN PEPPY

In the winter, frigid, biting winds often whip across the West Texas plains, making man and beast wish for thicker skin to halt the penetrating cold. The wind brings with it a continuous mist of floating sand. Neither

51

coats nor gloves can keep it from clinging to the eyes or grinding between the teeth. In fact, when the wind blows hard enough, sand seems to seep right through one's pores.

West Texas had its share of those kind of mornings the winter of 1971-1972 when Welch, having accomplished the goal of adding another NCHA Futurity trophy belt buckle to his collection, took over the reins of Mr San Peppy. After the excitement of exchanging Christmas gifts had mellowed, and the Christmas ornaments were stored for another year, Welch loaded Mr San Peppy into his trailer and headed for Odessa, Texas, to an AQHA-approved Junior cutting. It was the first time for Buster to show the stallion and Mr San Peppy won the class.

While maintaining a large cattle operation, with 4,000 partnership yearlings and 2,500 head of his own during the week, Welch began seriously hauling the horse on week-ends. When home, he polished Mr San Peppy's cutting skills on the fresh, fat cattle grazing on the lush, irrigated acres on which he partnered with S. J. Agnew. The hauling and polishing molded the stallion into an overnight success.

After the Odessa show, they traveled to the West Texas Maturity where again, Mr San Peppy took top honors. Weekend after weekend, the pair continued racking up earnings, along the way developing a deep mutual respect for one another. Every morning, Buster knew he was saddling an exceptional horse, one with great courage and ability; he also knew each time he rode him to the herd, that Mr San Peppy was main streaming his talent into 2 ½ minutes of unforgettable action.

In the early 70's, NCHA hosted only two aged events: the Futurity for 3-year-old horses and the Maturity, now called the Derby, for 4-year-old horses. With Buster on his back, Mr San Peppy, by then affectionately called "Peppy" by his trainer, swept the 3rd annual NCHA Maturity held in Albuquerque, New Mexico, April 1972, with a score of 224. Prior to the finals, he dominated the go-round performances with a combined score of 440, then earned a 219.5 to win the semifinals before tapping the finals off with his 224 run.

Shortly after winning the NCHA Maturity, Mr San Peppy had a new owner.

BUYING A STALLION

"After we won the Derby, I had a feeling that Mr. Howell might offer Peppy for sale," recalled Welch, "so I talked to S. J. Agnew about partnerin' with me if he became available. I estimated, by the horse market then, that Mr. Howell might want about $25,000 for him. Agnew said he'd partner with me and it wasn't long before Mr. Howell called me and said he wanted to sell the horse, but he had to have $50,000 for him.

"Well, that was quite a bit more than I'd told Jay Agnew, so Howell agreed to let us think about it for a few days, even offered to let us pay some down and pay it out as we liked. With that, I started trying to phone Jay, only to discover he'd gone to Europe!"

Uncertain as to whether Agnew would partner with him, since the going rate for Mr San Peppy doubled from his earlier estimation, Buster and his wife, Sheila, spent several days wrestling with the decision to either purchase the horse, realizing they might be sole owners, or let him go. One minute the answer was "no," it would be ridiculous to spend that much money on a horse, when $50,000 would buy a two-bedroom house and put a car in its garage. But the next moment, the answer was "yes," with Buster knowing he could not turn down the opportunity to own such an outstanding individual.

The couple talked about purchasing Mr San Peppy in the wee hours before dawn, they talked about him over lunch and talked about him when they retired at night. Then, Mr San Peppy made the decision for them.

"Nina, Sheila's daughter, was just a young little thing, but she could really ride a horse," said Buster. "I looked up one day, and she was out there close to the water trough workin' Peppy, my stirrups just a danglin'. It was the cutest thing to see so I yelled at Sheila, 'Look at that!' "

About the time Sheila glanced toward Nina, the cow that Peppy was working, circled around the end of the water trough.

"Peppy loped up to it and never hesitated," said Sheila, still with a look of amazement. "He just jumped the water trough, sat his hocks on the ground, turned around, and jumped back over the water trough. That cinched it."

Since Sheila and Buster's telephone was out of order, they went to their neighbors to call Mr. Howell. "Everyone in that family gathered 'round me in the kitchen when I placed that call," laughed Welch. "They'd never heard of anybody paying that kind of money for a horse, so they all listened while I worked out the deal with Mr. Howell."

Buster Welch and his wife Sheila moved to the King Ranch in the late 1970's. Photo courtesy of Buster and Sheila Welch.

Welch offered $15,000 down for Mr San Peppy, agreeing to pay the remainder of the purchase price over the next two years. "We were workin' that big operation, runnin' lots of steers, so I took some money from the ranch account and paid down on him," reminisced Welch. "I guess it was the cow man in me that refused to pay that much money all at one time for a horse, even as good a horse as that one. I wanted him to help pay for himself.

"We were really excited about it," he continued, "but the next morning, I woke up about 5:00 a.m., sat straight up in that bed, looked over at Sheila and yelled, '$50,000 dollars!' Then every morning, I'd wake up a little bit earlier, sit up in the bed and do the same thing."

Sheila laughed, remembering their early morning panic sessions. "We hadn't been married long, we had six kids living with us and we'd just bought a ranch with huge payments, so we had plenty of debt. We were young, though, and thought we were indestructible; scared, but indestructible."

When Agnew returned from Europe, Welch, after telling him he purchased Peppy while Agnew was gone, asked his ranching partner if he still wanted to buy half of the stallion. Without a moment's hesitation, Agnew answered, "Yep."

"I then told him, 'Now wait a minute, Jay; you'd better hear what I give for him.' But even after I told him I paid $50,000, he still said 'Yep' to the deal, sent me his half of the down payment and went on the note with me."

BUILDING A REPUTATION

Summer flourished in full force as the West Texas sun sent shimmering waves across the hot asphalt of the Texas highways. Buster Welch, however, barely noticed. It was time to go cutting; he had a stallion to promote. In a matter of days, he and Sheila loaded Mr San Peppy in their Miley trailer, specially built for Buster, and headed to cuttings in cooler California.

"At one of the first shows on the way to California, I marked a 77 on Peppy under George Tyler and that made me feel like I might have done the right thing. At the next show, Matlock Rose was judgin' and I marked a 78 under him. Matlock then followed me to the trailer and offered $80,000 for the horse. That took a big load off my shoulders after both those guys marked him like that and then Matlock offered that kind of money for him. I knew I'd done right by buyin' him."

As soon as one show ended, Welch headed for another one. The news of him and his hot stallion spread like wildfire through the cutting business, making its way to Texas in short time, even filtering down to King Ranch. Buster, however, wasn't the only one cashing in on the stallion's talents. Sheila also entered the arena on Mr. San Peppy, turning in her share of winning runs as well.

"He was awesome," described Sheila. "The first time I showed him, it started out as a lark, I didn't even have a hat on and my hair was flying everywhere. All I could think while I was riding him was 'Oh my gosh! He's going to stop and turn around! I've got to hang on!' "

In July, Buster and Peppy won the Pacific Coast Cutting Horse Association Maturity, once again sweeping all go-rounds. This time, the pair won the first go-round with a score of 149, tied for the first place in the second go-round with Doc's Starlight with a score of 149.5, and then won the finals with a score of 148. Welch pocketed $1,307.20 for the two-day competition.

1974 NCHA WORLD FINALS

November brought chilly nights, balmy days and the NCHA World Finals to Las Vegas. That first morning, as the yawning sun painted rustic hues against the mountains, hinting at an excellent day for cutting, Buster Welch walked quickly toward Mr San Peppy's stall, the fast walk an attempt to keep the morning cold from seeping into his bones. Along the way, he admired the early breaking dawn.

Welch had an appreciation for scenic mornings like that. They hinted of a rustic time long ago when Indians silhouetted the mountain ridges and buffalo roamed the plains below. Beautiful mornings, good reading, fat cattle and talented horses depicted a pretty good life to the rancher. Reaching Peppy's stall, he opened the door and quickly put the halter on him. Now though, it was time for work, time to get moving and let the beauty of the morning fade behind the business at hand.

Buster and Sheila had arrived at Horseman's Park in Las Vegas, Nevada, the day before, both of them prepared to show Mr San Peppy in the NCHA World Finals. While Sheila had inched up in the standings of the NCHA Non-Professional Top 10, a coveted way for any non-professional to end the year, Buster had to make this show count, should he accomplish the more difficult task of qualifying Mr San Peppy for the Top 10 standings in Open Competition, the class in which trainers competed.

He meant to do just that, although putting a horse in the Open Top 10 wasn't easy, especially when other obligations, like a ranching operation to run, a stallion to breed, horses to train, and a family to raise, hadn't allowed him to stay on the road all of the time.

Days later, however, when the World Championship finals ended, Buster had accomplished his goal. By winning $2,368.85, leading the Finals in money won, Peppy slipped into 10th place in the 1972 Open NCHA Top 10 contenders with total earnings of $5,572.35 for the year, only $30.10 behind 9th place, Missy's Hankie, owned by the So Ranch of Scottsdale, Arizona, and ridden by Mike Mowery.

In a sweeping victory, Sheila and Peppy shined in the Non-Professional Finals as well. The pair won both go-rounds and the finals, topping off the year with $2,171.45 and 7th place in the NCHA Non-Professional Top 10 Riders of 1972.

Mr San Peppy was not only paying his own way, he was making a name for himself as well.

7

NEW STALLION POWER

T he morning, like so many South Texas early dawns, offered a desert-like beauty to the dry, arid land as Tio Kleberg drove from his home in Kingsville to King Ranch. Deep in thought, however, the breaking day went unnoticed. Tio had other things on his mind. It was time to make a decision.

Tio liked what he knew about Mr San Peppy and he liked what he knew about the horse's rider, Buster Welch. Welch had placed the horse in the NCHA Top 10 and won the NCHA Derby as well in the last year. On top of that, he still managed to breed the stallion.

All of those pluses had Tio on a mission. He drove straight to the home of his cousin, Bobby Shelton, who, up and waiting for him, greeted Tio at the back door. The two men poured themselves a cup of coffee, then settled down for a deep discussion.

A few days later, Tio, Shelton and Stiles were leaning against a fence in Sweetwater, Texas, watching Buster Welch work horses.

"I told Bobby," voiced Tio, as he remembered that day, 'Look at this guy, he doesn't know what he's doing; he's using his reins and holding on to the saddle horn! We've been ridin' horses forever and we don't hold on like that.' "

With a sheepish grin spreading across his face that recounted how little he had understood about a trained cutting horse back then, he added, "In fact, I'd hoped I'd get a chance to ride and show that guy how to do it!"

Tio, Shelton and Stiles had just arrived at the Welch Ranch in Sweetwater, Texas. Unsure of where to go after parking the rent car, they had finally wandered over to the round pen to watch a man working his young colt. Earlier that year, Tio had heard about a young horse named Mr San Peppy that was making big waves in the cutting horse industry.

Kleberg had also learned that a rancher named Buster Welch, who trained horses as well, was part owner of the stallion receiving rave reviews in California, and that Welch stood the stallion in Sweetwater, Texas. After contacting Welch and setting up a time to see Mr San Peppy, he, Shelton and Stiles had flown to West Texas.

The stallion, described as an outstanding athlete by grapevine gossip, resembled a picture which had been developing in Kleberg's mind ever since he attended the NCHA Futurity. The ability of the horses he had witnessed at that show convinced him that buying or leasing a cutting horse was the ideal way to find a mate for King Ranch mares. Rather than visions of the stallion performing 2½ minutes of extraordinary skills in a cutting horse arena, however, Kleberg had visions of him siring outstanding foals crossed on King Ranch mares. Indeed, the three men had not flown across Texas to learn about a new hobby; their purpose was strictly business.

"A stallion has to have ability, conformation and pedigree to stand solid as a sire in a breeding program like King Ranch's," offered pedigree expert Larry Thornton of London, Arkansas. "Mr San Peppy fit those credentials;

the very fact that Mr San Peppy did carry the blood of King Ranch may have given him an edge in his ability to cross with King Ranch mares."

"Our objective from the beginning was to produce a better ranch horse; we never started out to breed a cutting horse," stated Kleberg. "Yet, the cutting horse was the kind of athlete that could do what we needed to do on the Ranch. Cutting horses displayed both the physical and mental ability that would help us gather our cattle. Bobby, Joe and I believed that if we found a sire with exceptional cutting qualities and bred him to our good broodmares, we would have better colts to use in our Ranch work."

For many years, Bobby Shelton heavily influenced the direction of the King Ranch Quarter Horse program. Photo courtesy King Ranch Archives, King Ranch, Inc.

In addition, Mr San Peppy's bloodline was linked to King Ranch breeding, an additional benefit that intrigued the men. Since Kleberg's younger days of 'quick-fix thinking,' he had come full circle, better understanding the strengths of line breeding. He now firmly believed that if they infused today's genetic knowledge with their line breeding program, the newer version of the old idea would produce a stronger, better product.

While Tio was scrutinizing the rider and voicing his opinion to Shelton, Welch was busily training a young horse in the arena, never looking up until he finished his work. As Kleberg watched the rider, who continually stopped the young colt, maneuvering frequently with two-hands, doubts swelled in his mind about what they had come to see, unaware that the man on the horse was Buster Welch. He had convinced Shelton and Stiles to make this trip and he hoped they weren't wasting their day.

60

When the training session ended, to Kleberg's surprise, the rider rode over to the fence and introduced himself as Buster Welch. Realizing that the man he had been watching was the same man he had come to see, Kleberg wondered again if perhaps they had made a dry run. Talk soon flowed easily between Welch and the three men, though, and Buster, an expert at asking the right questions, soon pinpointed the purpose of their mission.

"Those boys were wanting to get a good, modern breeding program going at King Ranch," explained Buster. "They had some of the greatest mares there had ever been down there, but they had neglected the breeding program for a while and they wanted to kind of 'jump-start' it."

"Now, I'd noticed," he continued slyly, "all of the big winning I'd done had been on King Ranch bloodlines, like Marion's Girl, for instance. I'd also won my third NCHA Futurity championship riding Rey Jay's Pete, which was sired by Rey Jay and Rey Jay was a King Ranch horse. That kind of winnin' on horses with their bloodlines made me interested in their program, too."

As Quarter Horse manager at King Ranch, Joe Stiles played a major role in the development of its Quarter Horse program. Photo courtesy King Ranch Archives, King Ranch, Inc.

Kleberg, Shelton and Stiles, yet to earn their wings on professional cutting horses, had come to look at the stallion with intentions of going home to discuss him. Welch, picking up vibrations of doubt, decided to put Kleberg horseback, believing that the best way to understand a cutting horse was to experience one. A good ride would not only be addictive, but would also remove any lingering hesitancy that the men might harbor about the athletic ability of cutting horses.

Glancing over his shoulder, Buster called to one of his hands. "Hey, go in there and get Sheila's horse and bring it back out here."

Minutes later, the employee appeared with a horse, still wet with sweat from a previous work, and handed the reins to Buster. Welch, with a smile, passed them on to Kleberg. "Here, you've done this a lot," he suggested, "why don't you try it for yourself?"

It was the moment the young man had been waiting for.

"We had watched Sheila work this horse earlier while we talked with Buster, and she looked like a china doll sitting up there, relaxed, no movement at all, so I felt this horse was a baby-sitter," grinned Tio, while shaking his head at the memory.

"I mounted, rode into the herd feeling very confident, cut a cow and all of a sudden, it all broke loose. That horse fell down in front of that cow, dancing back and forth, completely oblivious to me on his back. My feet flew in all directions, my head popped from side to side, and I hung on to that saddle horn until my hands hurt. I had not had one clue of what I had gotten into! I'd never SEEN a horse, much less FELT a horse, that turned that hard or rated a cow like that. Right then, I knew these were athletes."

MR SAN PEPPY

Welch saved the best for last. While Kleberg caught his breath from his first real ride on a trained cutting horse, Buster brought out Mr San Peppy. The stallion's appearance was everything the men had heard. Majestic in strength, he portrayed the image of a sire able to produce offspring capable not only of cutting out calves and heading off wild strays, but also of dragging them to the branding iron or holding an entire herd at bay.

Mr San Peppy also didn't disappoint them in the cutting arena. The stallion proved he had the talent to accompany the looks. With Buster on his back, rippling clouds of dust flew from beneath his hooves each time he fiercely thwarted the cow's move. Still, Kleberg and Shelton were leery to establish any long-range plans in such a short time.

"I had to sell them on Mr. San Peppy, on my program, my thoughts of where the horse business was going and what the future was for it. In fact, I think I did more selling than they did buying!" grinned Welch.

Buster's selling, however, worked. Before Kleberg, Shelton and Stiles left for King Ranch, and Buster left for more cuttings, a persuasive seller and an interested buyer agreed on breeding several King Ranch mares to Mr San Peppy. Again, King Ranch would be sending mares out, but this time the men felt they had narrowed the field, focusing on specific traits they needed in their horses to work cattle. Mr San Peppy had them.

"We liked what we saw, and I certainly liked what I felt, so we made the arrangement to send some mares to Mr San Peppy, and if we liked the foals, we would lease the horse from Welch and Agnew. We saw this as a great opportunity for us," admitted Tio.

Bobby Shelton cuts cattle at the King Ranch, a main activity in everyday Ranch work. Photo courtesy King Ranch Archives, King Ranch, Inc.

With dark clouds hanging over the cattle market, the opportunity to breed mares at King Ranch, and possibly later lease the stallion to them as well, smelled extra sweet to Welch. "I knew the cow market was fixing to break, and I didn't want to be buying any cattle right then so it worked out great for me, too."

Wanting to pick the best mares from their broodmare band to breed to Mr San Peppy, and knowing the value of Welch's lifetime of expertise with horses, Kleberg suggested he come to King Ranch and assist him and Stiles in selecting them. From his previous success with the King Ranch bloodlines, and being one who took pleasure in looking at great mares,

63

Welch graciously accepted the invitation to help choose what might best cross on Mr San Peppy.

PICKING MARES

From the days Captain King started ranching, improving the Ranch's horses was a major priority. In fact, King often paid more for horseflesh than he did for his land, realizing that the land was indeed worthless without good animals with which to work it.

"Life depended on having good horses," explained Helen Groves of the days of her great-grandfather. "There were no roads, only a few trails in those early days, so besides using horses to work with, they were the means of practical travel. Bandits and Indians also necessitated fast horses to catch up with them to recover stolen stock. Captain King knew the value of good horses and in one of his ledgers he shows the purchase of a Kentucky stallion for $500.00. That was at a time when land in the area was about 25 cents an acre."

Since the early 1900's, King Ranch had strived to develop a quality broodmare band to raise their own exceptional offspring, weeding out mares unable to produce colts better than themselves, bringing the better offspring back into the broodmare band to improve the next generation. It was a slow process with no shortcuts.

With time, however, a herd of mares appeared almost identical in size and color, and all of them were producers. By the time Welch joined the men of King Ranch to help them pick their better mares, many of the mares were 14 years old or older and had been producing colts for at least 10 years. King Ranch kept remarkable files on each mare: how her colts had fared in Ranch work, what were their strengths, their weaknesses, thus the strengths and weaknesses that the mare produced. The files resulted in an archive of information.

To the avid horseman enthralled with genetics, it was equine genealogy

64

at its best. Not only could the horseman observe the mare and her talents, he could also see a progression of her offspring, witnessing first-hand which genetic abilities she passed on to her foals year after year. It was a haven for study of generation after generation of one mare's produce, all on one ranch.

"We knew so much about our broodmares," remarked Tio. "We knew which mares produced colts with speed, which ones produced colts with more strength in their hindquarters, and which ones produce colts with other abilities. Studying this information, we congregated our best performance producing mares to breed to Mr San Peppy, trying to create the best offspring. That was in 1973. With Buster's help, we picked six of those we felt were the best and sent them to Mr San Peppy."

While the search for a stallion and the decision to breed to him had been a major arduous task for the young men, in the realm of King Ranch activity, it resembled the proverbial "drop in a bucket."

Reflecting back on that day, Stiles admitted, "We were just some young kids wanting to change 100 years of tradition. But, with over 300 mares on the Ranch and so much activity going on there all of the time, it wasn't like we were doing anything major by sending six mares off to be bred. You didn't even notice they were gone. We had no idea of the magnitude that this thing would turn into."

At that time, King Ranch, with its working cow operation, only wanted to find a stallion able to sire horses that could carry the *vaqueros* hour after hour on long hot days.

At that time, Buster Welch, a rancher and a trainer in Sweetwater, Texas, knew he had an exceptional product in Mr San Peppy, which could probably fulfill King Ranch's objective.

At that time, however, neither foresaw the impact that the stallion would make on all of their lives.

8

LEASING A STALLION

*I*t is not the critic who counts; not the man who points out how the strong man stumbled, or what the doer of deeds could have done better. The credit belongs to the man who is actually in the arena; whose face is marred by dust and sweat and blood; who strives valiantly; who errs and comes short again and again; who knows the great enthusiasms, the great devotions, and spends himself in a worthy cause; who at the best knows in the end the triumph of high achievement; and who at the worst, if he fails, at least fails while daring greatly; so that his place shall never be with those cold and timid souls who know neither victory nor defeat.

Theodore Roosevelt

After a few days at King Ranch helping to select mares, Welch returned home and continued the show career of Mr San Peppy, ending the 1973 year in fifth place in the NCHA's standings. For two years, the stallion had placed in the NCHA Top 10 as one of the best contenders in cutting. As a new year dawned, Buster decided it was time for Mr San Peppy to be the "best of the best." With his goal the 1974 NCHA World Championship, Welch checked the "Coming Events" in the *Cuttin' Hoss Chatter*, the official publicatin of the National Cutting Horse Association, for available cuttings, then headed west to the biggest one.

1974 WORLD CHAMPION

From the beginning, it was evident 1974 would be a good year. The pair started it off in rip-roaring style. With the first reporting of statistics in the April *Cuttin' Hoss Chatter*, Mr San Peppy led his competitors with earnings of $5,043.53; his closest competitor, Mr Sugar Boy, owned by Lee Holsey and ridden by Matlock Rose, was almost $800.00 behind him with earnings of $4,229.18. That was a sizeable lead since, in the early 70's, gas averaged 36 cents per gallon and a McDonald's hamburger could be purchased for 20 cents. (U.S. Postal Service 25th Anniversary Statistics.) The early months smelled heavily of success.

Mr San Peppy, however, had duties to perform other than hauling for the championship. There were mares to be bred so during the spring months, Buster took the stallion out of competition and home to Sweetwater to breed mares. The loss of time in the cutting arena took its toll, slipping him from first to fifth place.

By early summer, with all mares bred, Welch, undaunted by the standings, once again loaded his stallion and headed for a cutting, knocking away at the lead of those ahead of him. With Mr San Peppy's tumultuous fervor in the cutting arena, he passed one competitor then another in the standings, climbing the ladder to the number one spot. In the August *Cuttin' Hoss Chatter,* he had regained the lead, having won $10,152.20, and Two D's Dynamite sat second with $9,654 88. Welch, who liked a challenge, was determined to hold first place for the remainder of the year.

The year, however, offered more excitement than remaining in the number one spot. One sunny, warm California day, Buster and Sheila stopped at Denny's Restaurant in Indio, California, to eat.

"It was so hot at Indio," quipped Buster, "that when those 18 wheelers stopped, lizards climbed up on the exhaust pipe to cool their feet."

Buster parked the trailer in the shade of some trees, unloaded Peppy and Chickasha King, a gelding Sheila showed, and tied each of them to a side of the trailer while they ate. Later, as the two chatted happily while sauntering back to the truck, appetites satisfied and tea in their hands, Mr San Peppy initiated a test of Welch's cowboy abilities.

"We came out of that restaurant laughing, carryin' these two big ice teas to send us across the desert with, feeling good about the horses," recalled Welch. "About the time the trailer got in sight, Peppy, rubbing his head on the inline trailer's door handle, eased his halter off his head.

"There were 18 wheelers coming a 100 miles an hour down that highway and him loose, but he just started picking at the grass, so I sat my tea down, eased up there and got his halter. All the time, he's watchin' me. Just as I was ready to nab him, he picked up a crooked stick, cocked his head and stuck himself in the right side with that stick. Well, that was it; he was off and runnin'.

"Sheila threw her tea down and took off after him with me yellin' at her to not let him out of her sight. I ran around the trailer, untied Chickasha King's halter, but before I could jump on him bareback, he spooked and started going in circles. I had him by the mane, though, hangin' on; he's runnin' and spinnin' and my feet were flying' in the air, every once in a while bumpin' on the ground. Finally, he just sat down like a dog and when he did, I got on him and off we go.

"Course, by then, Sheila and Peppy were out of sight, but I heard him on the other side of some lumber stacked about 20 feet high, ready to be shipped. A railroad track ran parallel to the highway and that lumber was stacked in sections about 200 feet long for about a half mile. Between each section, there was break, so I got on this side of the lumber and rode as fast as I could, where he couldn't see me tryin' to get ahead of him. When we'd get to those breaks, though, I'd slow down to a trot because if he saw me runnin', he'd start runnin'.

"Finally, he got wind of all this anyway, threw his tail over his back and outrun me, goin' down between two big warehouses sittin' right on that highway. I knew I couldn't get behind him; if I did, I'd just run him straight into those 18 wheelers; so I went back around, and me and Chickasha King got out there runnin' down that highway, tryin to head him off, those trucks just whizzin' by us.

"When we finally rounded the corner of that warehouse, though, there he stood, about five feet from the highway, just peacefully grazing grass in a little area where water drained off the roof, like nothin' had happened. I slid off Chickasha King, walked right up to him and put the halter on him, got back on Chickasha King and started back to the trailer. Here came Sheila, runnin' and all out of breath, and I just rode right by her, didn't say a word, and grinned."

AN AGREEMENT

While Welch and Peppy continued to make a name for themselves in the arena, foals born on King Ranch sired by the stallion sealed Kleberg's desire to lease him. Mr San Peppy, having put his mark on his foals, helped their quality climb from "good" toward "superior."

"We flew into Abilene and met Buster there at the airport to talk about the deal," allowed Stiles. "Buster knew what he had and what he wanted; he was a good negotiator, tough but fair."

Tio agreed. "I was sitting on a bench at the airport, drinking an orange soda water, when we came to an agreement as to what we were going to do. We had been talking possibilities for a good while and had tossed around a number of ideas. It all finally jelled."

"I went down there to build a horse program," recalled Welch. "I just went for a year, ended up staying seven or eight, and kept the program going for 15 years. It was an interesting thing."

King Ranch leased Mr San Peppy and Welch became a part of that option as a consultant. In the October *Cuttin' Hoss Chatter*, King Ranch ran a full page advertisement:

> "We take pleasure in announcing that Buster Welch of Merkel, Texas, has been engaged to train some of our top cutting prospects. Buster will be associated with King Ranch in a program designed to train and develop the Old Sorrel family of Quarter Horses in the area that they were bred for... cutting and performance. We have also acquired the service of Mr San Peppy, a 1968 sorrel stallion by Leo San out of Peppy Belle. He will stand to outside mares during the 1975 breeding season at King Ranch-$1000."

By the time the year ended, Buster had new employment and King Ranch stepped out of tradition to breed to a new stallion. That stallion, Mr San Peppy, won the 1974 NCHA World Championship as well as the title of World Champion Cutting Horse Stallion. He also became the youngest horse to be inducted into the NCHA Hall of Fame.

SEPARATE PATHS, SIMILAR GOALS

"My father never met Buster Welch," recalled Helen Groves.

Bob Kleberg, a man who worked cattle in August 1974, was dead two months after Mr San Peppy's lease to King Ranch.

"While he was branding and working cattle that August," she continued, "he developed a terrible pain in his back but thought something was just 'out of kilter' as had happened numerous times before. It didn't get any better though. Eventually, he was operated on for cancer and died October

13, 1974."

By the time Kleberg died, Welch had become a part of King Ranch, but the two giants never met. "I saw him once," remembered Welch. "Somebody drove him by where we were working, but he was sick and didn't get out, and I didn't get over there before they left. I always hated that."

Groves saw many similarities between Welch and her father in their days on King Ranch, some good. some bad.

"Both had theories they worked under," analyzed Helen. "Both could do things with horses others couldn't do and both could bring out the best in people."

"On the other hand," she continued, "I didn't want to ride with my father on a four-lane highway. He was very apt to put on the brakes and go two lanes over if there was something he wanted to see, expecting the cars to go around him just as cattle in a herd would. He was used to cattle giving way to him, and thought other things, like cars, would go round him, too. Buster drove that way, too."

Like Kleberg, Welch did prefer the land to a growing, modernized world, and like Kleberg, he, too, believed he could best make his money horseback. Therefore, the call to King Ranch, a Ranch that still adhered to old ways; a Ranch that ended in part where the sea began, fit the man who preferred the ways of people living 100 years earlier.

9

A TRANSITION ERA

"*W*hatever you can do, or dream you can, begin it.
Boldness has genius, power and magic to it.*"

Goethe

The energy of a new era flourished on King Ranch in the late 70's. For the first time in generations, an outside stallion had been leased and now stood on its soil. With his father's health declining, Tio Kleberg assumed more of the administrative responsibilities of the Ranch, and, in addition, a commercial breeding operation escalated like wildfire.

FIRST, A RANCH

Even with all of the change, King Ranch remained, first and foremost, a working Ranch symbolized by *vaqueros*, Santa Gertrudis cattle and sorrel horses. As they had every morning for generations, Ranch headquarters bustled with activity long before the sun rose as the cow boss, the windmill crew and the fence crew gathered for an early morning cup of coffee and received their orders for the day. Also, as they had every morning for generations, the crews dispersed by daylight to fix broken windmills, mend fences and move cattle.

Moving horses on King Ranch. Photo courtesy King Ranch Archives, King Ranch, Inc.

While the addition of a new stallion and a trainer represented the dawning of a fresh era, the past, itself, remained the same. The new birth joined a firm foundation of tradition as old as the West. Many of those of the old tradition, wary of change, watched the new ideas vigilantly, uncertain of a break with past customs. Welch wisely proceeded within the roots of King Ranch philosophy.

"I wanted to keep it ranchy," remarked Welch about the horse program he established on King Ranch. "Although the horse market was good at that time, having experienced its casualty rate before, I didn't believe it would stay that good very long, so I didn't want to spend a bunch of money and create something that wouldn't fit with ranching. Should it not work, I wanted them to be able to turn whatever we did back to ranching."

Behind the Santa Gertrudis Ranch headquarters, where once exquisite Thoroughbred horses with high-strung dispositions pranced, a long horse barn, still referred to as the Thoroughbred Barn, became home to Quarter Horses now in cutting training. At one time, Thoroughbreds had reigned on King Ranch, introduced there in the late 30's by Bob Kleberg.

Kinenos during a memorial service for Dick Kleberg, Jr., at King Ranch included (l to r) Miguel Muniz, Encarnacion Silva Jr (Chon), Manuel Silva, Rogelio Silva, a riderless horse, Martin Mendietta Jr., Julian Buentello, Roberto Mendietta Sr. (Beto), Francisco Montalvo (Pancho), Jaime Quintanilla, Valentine Quintanilla (Lente), Nicolas Rodriquez (Pacho), Eubense Garza, Jorge Mayorga (Choche). Not shown is Javiel Quintanilla who worked for Mr. Dick for over 35 years. Photo courtesy King Ranch Archives, King Ranch, Inc.

Like Tio, only years before him, Bob, also searching for bloodlines to improve the Ranch's breeding program, had turned to Thoroughbreds for breeding stock. The Thoroughbreds soon became a King Ranch sport as well, and the great stallion, Assault, thrust the Ranch into racing history, winning the prestigious 1946 Triple Crown. Today, the coveted Triple Crown trophy remains regally on display on the dining table in the Main House.

SHOWING

With exposure to a new activity on the Ranch, it was only a matter of time before work drifted over to play. At first, several King Ranch shareholders merely flirted with cutting competition while Welch was inaugurating his training program, but before long, the infatuation turned to addiction.

Buster Welch in a herd of Santa Gertrudis at King Ranch. Photo courtesy King Ranch Archives, King Ranch, Inc.

Soon Welch was giving cutting lessons and carrying new non pros to weekend competitions. However, Ranch horses remained his top priority, so rather than request a new horse trailer for hauling, he relied on his own McQuerry Trailer to get horses to the show. Using this specially built convertible stock trailer, christened `Ol Blue', he would load the horses of his new non-pros, along with Mr San Peppy for himself to show, and head for a cutting.

"I got it in 1962," relived Buster of the trailer's birth. "Mike McQuerry made it for me so I could either haul cattle or petition it and haul six horses. It has these little hooks next to the roof and straps so you can buckle the partitions up there. I probably used it hauling cattle more than horses."

Then with eyes smiling, he added, "We've still got it, but you can just barely find blue paint on it now."

While a Cadillac trailer of its day, unlike the shiny, immaculate trailers that only hauled horses and traveled mainly asphalt highways, the body of Welch's trailer told tales of true ranch life. A dent here and there announced the meeting of metal with rugged West Texas rocks; long claw marks on its sides showed the fight from brush and mesquites against the trailer's invasion into their domain, and other knocks and dimples acknowledged where scrambling calves had left their marks both inside and out.

For all of its dents, scrapes, nicks and loss of paint, Ol' Blue still looked better parked along side the shiny rigs at arenas around Texas than any trailer King Ranch owned. Grinning, Joe Stiles reiterated the choices available during the transition days for hauling horses to shows.

"If you remember, King Ranch had pretty well been a self-contained Ranch and had no need for trailers to haul horses away from there," reminded Joe. "We had a goose neck trailer or two that showed so much wear and tear from bouncing across miles of rough land and holding rough livestock that they made Buster's "Ol' Blue" look like a million dollars. I can also remember a wooden trailer and a Dodge Power wagon that pushed through the brush and, of course, a big cattle truck, but that was the extent of our machinery.

"We hadn't been taking horses off the Ranch, so King Ranch hadn't had any need for fancy rigs. In fact," added Joe as an afterthought, "we'd just barely passed the era when we rode horses everywhere!"

Tio Kleberg. Cindy Yamanaka: Dallas Morning News.

As with the Thoroughbred days, when horses bought to purposely enhance Ranch bloodlines also eventually encouraged a sport, before long, the Quarter Horse program followed in its footsteps. In reality, cutting as work, and cutting as a sport, worked hand-in-hand. Kleberg and Stiles had learned money could not buy advertisement equal to that of a good performing horse when they had roamed the All-American Congress in search of potential horses. Therefore, they knew a good King Ranch cutting horse in the arena could be their best advertisement. Now, with improved bloodlines and with several Ranch shareholders interested in cutting horses, it was a natural progression that horses to show at cutting competitions followed on the heels of breeding and training horses for Ranch work.

"When we started seeing the talent of these individuals," explained Kleberg, referring to better-bred horses, "It made sense to earmark some of them for competition. Obviously, out of the horses you train, only one or two percent will make the grade for shows, but the remainder of the horses which had been in training with that one or two percent, made outstanding Ranch horses."

There was even a side benefit to training show horses since it offered an excellent method for culling inferior Ranch horses as well. A colt, unable to stand the rigors of cutting horse training, could never hold up to the intense pressures of gathering and sorting calves at a roundup. For that, one needed stronger hips and more mental stamina than what was needed for just 2 1/2 minutes.

Moving King Ranch cattle. Photo courtesy King Ranch Archives, King Ranch, Inc.

As the program grew, the back of the practice arena at King Ranch became more crowded as lopers weaved in and out among each other, loping the fresh edge off of their horses while waiting their turn with Welch. When the trainer finished working one horse, he stepped off of it, handed the reins to an employee and immediately stepped onto a fresh horse. The pattern continually repeated itself throughout the morning. For every good side, however, there can be a down side. While training for sport took on more importance, a balancing act ensued to retain the principal objective of developing good Ranch horses.

"There's a certain line between a competition horse and a ranch horse," said Kleberg. "Some competition horses wouldn't last a week at the Ranch. They're not big enough; you couldn't rope a 1,200-pound cow on them. While training for competition would provide us with the talent for good working Ranch stock, we couldn't forfeit strength and size with our horses."

COMMERCIAL BREEDING

While reconstructing their horse program, Kleberg recognized potential from Mr. San Peppy's prosperity for opening a door for a commercial breeding program. He also realized, should they wish to pursue the new business, it was up to the people of the Ranch to make it work. Rather than languish in past laurels, if they wanted to stand Mr San Peppy to outside mares, every day counted in planning a superb marketing strategy to promote him.

As Welch focused on evaluating the King Ranch colts that first year, Mr San Peppy stood to several outside mares. To the surprise of Kleberg, when King Ranch threw open its gates to outside breeding in 1975, the public responded enthusiastically. A year later, when foals dotted pastures throughout the country, 55 of them were registered with the American Quarter Horse Association as sired by Mr San Peppy. They were testimony to the success of the first King Ranch commercial breeding program since the number almost doubled from the previous year's registrations.

"This was our first time to stand to outside mares and, therefore, our first exposure to commercial breeding" recalled Tio. "We did this because Buster's theory was to breed Peppy to as many mares as we could, believing that the more good mares you bred to, the more opportunity you had for good colts to be trained. I had a hard time understanding that concept since it seemed opposite of 'supply and demand.' Buster, however, was a proponent of exposure to the best mares available; we just didn't know who the best mares were at that time to cross on him."

Welch also suggested King Ranch find good sons of Mr San Peppy and promote several of them, which, in turn, would promote Mr San Peppy. Therefore, in December 1976, in Fort Worth, Texas, only a month after Mr San Peppy won his second NCHA World Championship, taking home saddles, blankets, buckles, trophies and even the use of a one-ton Chevrolet pickup for a year, and after King Ranch had exercised its option to purchase the stallion, Welch and Kleberg strolled up and down the aisles of the sale barn searching the NCHA Futurity consignees, looking for offspring of Mr San Peppy. Liking what they saw, King Ranch purchased two sons of

Mr San Peppy, as well as several Mr San Peppy fillies.

"Although we had some colts of our own on the ground by then, none of them were old enough to put in training," continued Kleberg. "Buster was breaking eight or 10 of them, but they weren't sired by Peppy. They were out of our broodmares and we were trying them just so we could see what kind of talent we might get from the broodmare side."

Wanting to once again have a top-quality breeding program at King Ranch, the men did their homework. Already, 2,500 head of horses stood on King Ranch soil from which to select broodmares, but rather than make judgment calls only by physical appearances, Kleberg, Welch and Stiles relied also on age and ability, spending long hours researching past records which had been meticulously kept by King Ranch.

"Joe, Tio and I went to those divisions and went through the *remudas* picking out some of the good, young mares, as well as some of the older ones," remembered Welch. "The cowboys had a tendency to keep ridin' the old ones they liked rather than develop their young horses. We needed those good older mares in the broodmare band, though, so they could produce more foals just like themselves. We took 700 horses out of those *remudas* before it was over."

Picking out mares that had eye appeal was just the first step in broodmare band development. Combining that eye appeal with hard facts about the mare's ability became the second assignment.

"We studied pedigrees," he continued. "We went back through records that Mr. Dick and Mr. Bob Kleberg had written on these horses and the comments they had made. Those men had ridden these horses and cut cattle on them day in and day out so they knew the best cow horse bloodlines."

Both Kleberg and Stiles were both proficient students of the horses on King Ranch, which proved a great asset in evaluating such a large number of horses. What they did not know about them or if they could not find something about them in records, they knew which older *vaqueros* to visit to acquire the needed knowledge. The *vaqueros,* who spent more time with their horses than their wives, knew horseflesh. They knew which ones excelled, their little quirks and the ones with bad temperaments that needed to be culled.

Combining all of this information provided an abundant array of knowledge. By the time the long exhausting hours of gathering and classifying data had ended, Kleberg, Stiles and Welch knew which King Ranch bloodlines had done well.

Still, rather than rely only on their breeding program, King Ranch also sent many of its mares to be bred to other stallions to generate new bloodlines on the mare side. Fillies born to these matings provided mares to then breed to King Ranch stallions in years to come. In addition, King Ranch purchased mares to compliment those of exceptional breeding they already owned.

"We got a chance to buy some of Jay Agnew's good mares," added Welch. "Jay was an astute horseman who always said the only Thoroughbred that hurts a cutting horse is what they don't have. He'd bring those Thoroughbred mares off the track and try to find one that had some cow in her. He found one pretty, bald-face mare, a mile-and-half stakes mare, that had cow in her, and she produced some good horses."

The Thoroughbred mare, Fairway's Gal, produced Tenino Fair, which, in turn, produced Badge of Courage, Tenino San, and Little Tenino. Welch also found a keeper in the mares they had culled. Having missed being bred for a couple of years, the mare had been eliminated from the broodmare band.

"I drove down one evening and just sat in my pickup and watched the mares move around, and this one caught my eye," mused Welch. "She was a Rey Del Rancho mare, and she just had a look about her. I liked the way she moved and stopped and handled herself. She just looked like one who could stop and turn. I was high on the Rey Del Rancho bloodline anyway, so that made me really like her."

NEW HELP

Welch had met Steve Knudsen in 1974, while hauling Mr San Peppy for his World Championship title. At that time, the Amarillo Cutting Horse Association hosted quite a few cuttings with high-dollar stakes, as did several other associations in northern Texas and surrounding states. To make the shows, but still tend to his work at King Ranch, Welch left Mr San Peppy at Stanley Glover's ranch in the hands of Glover's employee, Steve Knudsen.

"Ol' Steve was a good guy," recalled Buster. "He was

Steve Knudsen moved to King Ranch, where he still works today. He is shown here recently with Little Peppy. Photo by Janell Kleberg

a hard worker and really dependable; the kind of guy you'd like to have taking care of your horses, so I told Stanley that if Steve ever wanted to leave him, to send him to me."

In September, after the Colorado State Fair, Welch loaded Mr San Peppy and returned to Kingsville, and shortly thereafter, Knudsen went home to South Dakota. Glover shared with Welch the fact that Knudsen might be available to work.

"Buster called on a Sunday and asked if I'd be interested in coming to work on King Ranch," said Knudsen. "I thought about it and knew it would be great on my resume to have both trained under Buster and worked for King Ranch. So when he called me back the next Thursday, after talking with Tio about hiring me, I told him that I'd be down the next week."

Knudsen, although hired to break and ride colts, was soon handling the stallions for the breeding program. Besides standing Mr San Peppy, King Ranch also stood El Pobre and Otoes Hand. Knudsen handled the breeding stallions until the Ranch closed down the breeding operation in 1992. Since he still works for King Ranch, he has yet to use his resume.

El Pobre, a foundation stallion that stood at King Ranch. Photo courtesy of King Ranch Archives, King Ranch, Inc.

A NEW PRACTICE

With the new era, King Ranch experienced its own technological revolution. In the past, stallions "pasture bred" the mares, but with the influx of outside mares to be bred, pasture breeding by Mr San Peppy was not an option. With the new stallion on the Ranch, and following the new program for culling colts, King Ranch employees had to adapt to a new breeding program entrenched with modern technology. As trailer after trailer pulled through the gate delivering mares ready for breeding, the old method of pasture breeding, at least for Mr San Peppy, took a back seat to artificial insemination. But it wasn't without its hitches.

Artificial insemination for equines wasn't a routine method of breeding when King Ranch veterinarian Dr. Jerry Morrow went to vet school, but he quickly adapted to the program. To insure that the mares were ready to be bred, stallions were used to "tease" the mares, which usually excited the stallions as well. For that reason, as well as the fear of risking injury, only stallions not on the show roster made the teasing roster.

Or so Buster thought. One morning, as he drove into the Ranch ready to load horses for a week-end show, he casually glimpsed toward Morrow teasing the mares in preparation for breeding. Welch immediately slammed on the brakes for a better look. Sure enough, the snorting stallion with his tail in the air was Mr San Peppy which Morrow had grabbed in haste to get the breeding done.

A SECOND CROWN FOR MR SAN PEPPY

The 1975 breeding season, even with its glitches, firmly established King Ranch's commercial breeding operation as a resounding success and a financial boon to its equine program. Knowing the more laurels around Mr San Peppy's neck, the better the program would be, Welch decided to once again haul Peppy for a second World Championship. Showing provided the ideal way to expose the stallion to a targeted breeders' market.

With the announcement in the April **Cuttin' Hoss Chatter's** NCHA standings, Mr San Peppy sat firmly in first place with $7,758.17, almost $2,500.00 ahead of his closest competitor, Jay Freckles owned by Jim and Mary Jo Milner of Ft worth and shown by Bill Freeman. Even though Mr San Peppy was standing to mares at King Ranch, now that Buster had additional help to haul the horse to and from shows, while he often flew to them, Mr San Peppy's earnings kept climbing instead of falling behind, as he had done in 1974.

By May 23, he had won $11, 711.14; three months later his earnings had more than doubled to $27,458.34. In Amarillo, Texas, on November 6, 1976, Mr San Peppy received his second World Championship title, along the way setting a new one-year earnings record for an open cutting horse of $34,065.61.

Rey del Rancho, another King Ranch stallion. Photo by Glenn Cisco.

He also added to his ever-increasing list of credentials, the honor of being the only stallion to ever win the World Championship twice.

84

KING RANCH'S CROWN JEWEL

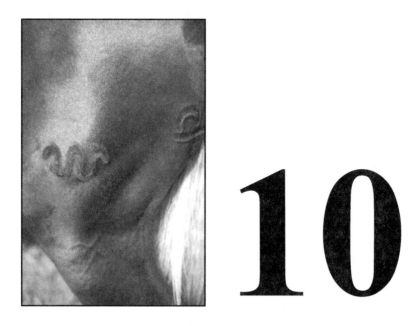

10

MEETING PEPPY SAN BADGER

*T*io Kleberg stood on the outside of the arena, one boot resting on the fence, hands shoved into pants pockets, enjoying the earthy aroma of horse sweat and dust. It was a nostalgic smell, one that always reminded him of his childhood roundup days. Behind him the roar of the lawn mower manicuring the Santa Gertrudis headquarters lawn muffled periodic whinnies of horses and the conversations of the Ranch hands going about their daily routine.

Tio thought the myriad of activity amazing. Buster, persuading a 3-year-old to do things his way inside the arena, however, was totally unaware of the hustle and bustle of activity surrounding him. Sights, sounds and smells vied for attention from every direction, yet to Welch, absorbed in his project, none of it existed.

None of it had a couple of years ago.

Several hands loped colts in the back of the arena; another crossed the road toward him with a fresh colt to be loped, while still one more led a lathered sorrel back to the barn. Tio slowly took it all in. Gazing past the lawn where a crew busily swept sidewalks and picked up grass clippings, remnants of the deafening lawn mower, he watched more young hands bathing and brushing still more young horses.

Kleberg liked what he saw. He liked the hustle and bustle, the smell of horses, the sound of horses, the sight of horses. In the 2 ½ years since Buster Welch had joined them, the master horseman had spearheaded an immense change on King Ranch. The importance of horses headed the list, having unintentionally drifted to the back-burner in previous years. Now, though, they demanded priority status.

Pulling a hand free from his pocket, he glanced at his watch; already, he was short on time. With a last look at the menagerie of horse work, he turned and climbed into his car. It was time to leave for Amarillo. He had his own horse work which to attend.

As the meeting of the American Quarter Horse Association Board of Directors adjourned, Joe Kirk Fulton, a previous halter and cutting horse breeder, now inclined toward racing, moved around the room to visit with Tio Kleberg. Fulton, whose ranch was in Lubbock, Texas, knew about King Ranch's search for offspring of Mr San Peppy and he believed he had one of the stallion's best 3-year-olds standing in his barn.

"I told Tio that I had one heck of a colt by Mr San Peppy at the Ranch," remembered Fulton. "I'd sent my good mare, Sugar Badger, to breed to Mr San Peppy and got this colt. He showed talent from the first time Bruce Reeves, who worked for me, started him," said Fulton.

Kleberg had heard this kind of story before since all owners, like parents with children, felt their Mr San Peppy offspring was outstanding. He was still searching for exceptional colts, however, knowing somebody out there had to have one, so he listened intently as Fulton talked about the horse.

"Bruce had done an excellent job of starting the colt, but he wasn't a trainer, and, therefore, he was inexperienced at finishing him," continued Fulton. "Tio and I talked about horses for awhile and then I asked him about sending Bruce and the colt, Peppy San Badger, down to King Ranch for a couple of days. I'd pay their keep down there if his trainer, Buster Welch, would spend a little time with Bruce, making sure he was headed in the right direction."

For King Ranch, it was important for the advertisement of their stallion that all of Mr San Peppy's colts receive good training. The more his colts excelled in the show arena, the more the demand for breeding to Mr San Peppy would certainly escalate. Kleberg graciously invited Fulton to send the cowboy and Peppy San Badger to King Ranch.

Peppy San Badger had star credentials. Besides his famous father, his dam, Sugar Badger, was a proven producer, as well as a granddaughter of Grey Badger III. Fulton knew teaming with Kleberg to provide Reeves with intensive instruction would benefit both parties; he would have a better trained stallion out of the arrangement and, should Peppy San Badger do well at shows, the stallion would be the best kind of advertisement for his sire and King Ranch.

THE BIRTH OF THE LEGEND

Ironically, Buster Welch, who had recently heard about the colt, was in part responsible for Peppy San Badger being born. Several years earlier, while at the Dallas Fair cutting, an encounter with Wayne Pooley, who was then training horses for Fulton, encouraged the breeding.

"Buster and I were standing in the middle of the arena talking," remembered Pooley. "I'd tied my turn back horse to the fence, but Buster was holding Mr San Peppy. About that time, a guy I was supposed to turn back for yelled at me as he rode toward the herd. I'd forgotten all about it. I started to run for my turn-back horse and Buster said, 'Here, use Mr San Peppy.' Well, I thought he was kidding, since he hadn't even shown yet, so I

88

started off again, but he insisted and handed me the bridle reins, so I jumped on him and turned back for the guy."

Although Welch was leading the cutting on Mr San Peppy at that time, he had no qualms about the stallion working as a turn-back horse before he showed him again. In fact, Welch, himself, used him frequently as his turn-back horse. The loan proved profitable. Pooley, who already liked Mr San Peppy, was even more enamored after he had ridden the horse, and upon returning him to Buster, discussed breeding Sugar Badger, a good mare that Fulton owned, to him. Back at home, he shared the story with Fulton and the two men agreed that Sugar Badger and Mr San Peppy might be a good cross.

"Peppy San Badger was born in 1974, and since Joe Kirk was phasing out his show horse operation, I left there on February 15, 1976," said Pooley. "At that time, I'd never been on the colt. He'd had distemper and been pretty sick, so all I'd done was saddle him and put him on the walker; I never even got him broke. Reeves, who was wagon boss at the other Ranch, moved over when I left."

Pooley's oldest son, Richard, continued to work for Fulton, so Pooley returned periodically for visits. On a return visit during Thanksgiving, nine months later, the young stallion he had left behind impressed him.

"Bruce asked me to ride Peppy San Badger. I loped him around a little bit, and then I worked that dude and I've never ridden a 2-year-old that tried as hard and would hold a cow like that one. I've ridden some good 2-year-olds; in fact, we used to show 2-year-olds, but he was the most dynamic one I'd ridden. We're talking about a 2-year-old stud, and he was plenty nice. Bruce had never trained a horse for competition or shown one for cutting, but he'd ridden a million good ranch horses and he'd done a really good job on Peppy San Badger."

Later, Fulton arrived and again Pooley rode the stallion, finding him to be as good, if not better, the second time. He, therefore, began talking to his friend about buying the horse.

"I kept telling Joe Kirk he ought to sell me that horse," said Pooley, "but he said 'No, I'm going to send him to the big ranch; we're going to use this one as a ranch stud.' I just didn't want that to happen so I kept talking to him, but he wouldn't sell him."

The following spring, Buster and Joe Stiles took their 3-year-olds to Brinks Ranch where Pooley was then employed to work their horses. "They were both riding Mr San Peppy colts," remembered Wayne, "and we got to talking about them. I told 'em I'd seen the best Mr San Peppy colt there was and may ever be. I reminded Buster of that time at the Dallas Fair when I'd ridden Mr San Peppy and told him this was the colt from that breeding."

REEVES AND PEPPY SAN BADGER

In Lubbock, Texas, years of cowboying for a living proved to be the teacher for Reeves as he worked with Peppy San Badger. Instinctively, he molded the colt with gentle encouragement rather than forcing ways on him. The method worked, although at the time, Reeves didn't realize that there even was a method. He was particularly proud of his protegee, especially since he considered himself a cowboy, and, in no way, a horse trainer.

"I knew what he should do and kind of what he should look like doing it, but I didn't consider myself a trainer," acknowledged Reeves. "I mainly tried to keep him from picking up bad habits. He actually broke himself, and I went along for the ride."

Bruce Reeves started Peppy San Badger, the stallion that later became known as Little Peppy to the cutting horse industry. Photo courtesy of Buster and Sheila Welch.

90

Reeves used a square pen, *Corriente* roping steers, and a hit-and-miss riding program as his tools to mold Peppy San Badger. Since Ranch work saddled him with more duties than training the young stallion, days passed when Peppy San Badger never felt a bit in his mouth. Besides every-day Ranch care, Reeves spent hours on the road hauling horses back and forth between Fulton's San Marcos Ranch and his Lubbock Ranch, and making frequent hauls to the race tracks in Ruidoso. His work made developing a daily regime on the horse, which was like "play time," impossible.

"When I'd come home, I'd just ride him real good that day," recalled Reeves. "It was fruitless to work him; you could work him the next day, but not the first one. When I was home, though, he was a thrill to be on. I often rode him in the early morning and again late in the evening. One time I'd work him, then the next time I'd lope him out in the cotton fields. I also took him to ropings with me and let midnight hit him in the top of the head," he continued. "I'd tie him to a trailer and just leave him there until the ropin' was over, which was usually 1:00 or 2:00 a.m. That helped his attitude the next day; but it didn't help mine, necessarily."

Peppy San Badger had a spirit about him that Reeves admired. "He was a buckin' son of a gun in the beginning. Every time you got on him, he'd buck three or four times, but it wasn't mean buckin'; he wanted to be good. Later, as he got used to things; you could hold him and he wouldn't buck."

Musing for a moment about the days of breaking Peppy San Badger, Reeves added, "Bet he'd buck today if you stepped on him and rile him; he just had that temperament. That's what made him so good, though, that and his heart was so big."

A TRIP TO KING RANCH

Shortly after Fulton returned home from his AQHA meeting, about the time March winds, howling across the Texas plains, made one pull his coat tighter, Reeves rose in the wee hours of the morning and loaded Peppy San Badger, along with his dam, Sugar Badger, which was returning to the court of Mr San Peppy. By daylight, he was already miles down the road toward King Ranch and a warmer part of Texas. Like a proud father, he was anxious to show off his young colt. He was especially anxious to hear how Buster Welch might evaluate the colt.

"Now that was a mistake!" laughed Reeves looking back to 1977. "If I'd known then what I know now, I'd never have worked that sucker except in the dark. Nobody would've known how good he was until the show. But he loved his job, and I loved to let him do it, and I loved to show him off. I guess in the end, it was the best for all of us."

For Tio, when Peppy San Badger arrived at King Ranch, he was just another horse among many. The stallion's entry into the arena, however, and his acceptance of his new surroundings, attracted his attention.

"Joe Stiles, Steve Knudsen, and I were sitting in the arena when Bruce showed up," said Tio. "We had four or five concrete steps that led down into the arena, and rather than go around and come in the gate, Reeves just rode Peppy San Badger down those steps. Even though he was a young horse in new surroundings, he didn't back up or jump out, he just walked down into the arena as if there was nothing to it. We all took notice of that. That proved Bruce had him real broke, but he was also real green."

For the next several days, Reeves alternated with Welch in working his stallion. He watched the trainer's hands while listening carefully to every word he said, wanting to saturate himself with training ideas so he might help his colt. While Reeves concentrated on absorbing his training lessons, word spread quickly around the Ranch that the new colt down for a "visit" was worth watching.

"I held herd in the arena while Bruce cut a cow on this horse the first day," recalled Joe. "He was the prettiest-moving horse I'd ever seen; he looked like a ball of mercury going across the pen. It didn't make any difference that nothing was done correctly; he just moved so pretty that he reached out and grabbed you. Bruce had done an excellent job of breaking him and starting him."

"Everybody liked him," acknowledged Welch. "Everybody thought he was a nice colt, and I thought he was a nice colt, too." Then, with the wisdom that comes from sitting in the saddle so many years, he added, "There's no cinch in this business, though, but the cinch on your saddle, and a time or two in my life I've had them to break."

Still, for all his ineptness with procedure, the young stallion made a splash with his classy physical appearance. To those on King Ranch accustomed to complete sorrel horses, the splash of blaze on his face and the white on his legs made Peppy San Badger an eye catcher.

For several days, Welch worked the colt, coaxing from him the "feel" that only a horseman of his caliber could find in an inexperienced colt. As he cut one cow and then another on the young stallion, Peppy San Badger relayed to his rider an intense mixture of desire and ability, clothed with flowing motion rather than the tumultuous moves of his father. At that time, promoting Mr San Peppy ranked number one in priorities at King Ranch, so thoughts crowded Welch's mind that this offspring might be an "ace in the hole" for promoting the sire.

Relying heavily on Welch's expertise to guide them, Stiles and Kleberg also eyed the Ranch visitor as a possible means for promoting Mr San Peppy. Still, the merging dream of using Peppy San Badger as a promotional package had its obstacles.

First, the stallion was owned by someone else, so King Ranch had little control over his destiny. Secondly, the young stallion, although extremely well broke, was still in kindergarten compared to the cutting training received by other colts being readied for the Futurity. This lack of training made flickering doubts roam in the minds of Kleberg and Welch. Kleberg wondered if there was still enough time to ready Peppy San Badger for the event, harboring no illusion that the stallion could win the crown.

In addition, it bothered Kleberg that Joe Kirk Fulton had, for the most part, left cutting behind to concentrate on his fascination with the racing industry. Since Fulton wasn't attached to the sport anymore, should Peppy

San Badger not do well at the Futurity, he might lose interest and no longer aggressively promote him. It made no difference how great a horse he was; if Peppy San Badger wasn't promoted, he would not enhance Mr San Peppy's breeding stature.

That happened at futurities. Many a good horse never made the second go. It might be the cattle, the draw, or the nerves of both the horse or rider; there were so many variables in cutting. The cream of the crop could easily lose the race before the first lap. Kleberg, however, never put all his money on one show; the Futurity was just the first of many and if this horse was their "ace in the hole," Tio didn't want to chance losing it.

Early one morning, before the day totally awakened with activity and the chirp of birds could still be heard, Kleberg and Reeves slowly walked their horses in a circle, more engrossed in talking with one another than the daily perfunctory lope used to take the edge from horses.

"I asked Bruce what he thought Joe was going to do with Peppy San Badger after the Futurity," explained Kleberg. "He kind of shrugged and told me he imagined Fulton would put him out on one of his ranches."

His reply disturbed Kleberg. Perhaps King Ranch should try to buy the horse to insure he was shown, but as he watched Reeves with Peppy San Badger, Reeves concerned him also. He carried in his heart more than the normal affection a cowboy has for a horse. That kind of attachment didn't come along very often. It was almost sacred, and almost immoral to consider dissolving it.

As soon as Reeves return to Lubbock, Welch, Stiles, and Kleberg gathered at headquarters to discuss the new Mr San Peppy offspring. The men discussed the exceptional potential Welch believed, but could not guarantee, the colt had. They discussed the horse's mental ability paired with his physical ability, his new style of working and the charisma he had to make it all appear effortless. Then, they discussed how far behind he was in training.

Still, Welch thought Peppy San Badger had the sparkle of a champion hiding inside him and that he should be a success in the arena at some time or another, if given the opportunity. His success would then boomerang to his sire, and that was the ultimate goal.

Decisions rarely come easy, especially when planning a future that carries no guarantees. After a long discussion, the three men agreed that if there was a chance Fulton might put the stallion out to pasture after the Futurity rather than show him, then King Ranch should try to buy him and promote him themselves. Peppy San Badger could help prove Mr San Peppy as a breeding stallion. Kleberg, thinking about Reeves' affection for the horse, decided if the horse could be purchased, it had to be done without any ill will.

Reeves felt in his bones that King Ranch was interested in Peppy San Badger. He approached Fulton about his concern. Fulton, however, having heard nothing from King Ranch, assured Reeves he planned to keep the 3-year-old.

"After I got home, though, Buster called me every day asking about him," commented Reeves.

Several days later, Tio placed a call to Joe Kirk. "We were down in the Vet Office and I didn't get anywhere with that first call; he didn't want to sell him. In fact, he wanted to show him in the futurity in his name."

The refusal to sell did not discourage the men. Welch also talked with Fulton on several occasions, attempting to find out exactly how Fulton wanted to sell the horse. "Joe Kirk priced the horse at $50,000 and that was 'cuttin' a big fat hog' back then. It would be like giving $200,000 or more for a horse today. I talked to him two or three times, trying to negotiate this thing. At that time, King Ranch was suspicious of purchasing any outside horses, since they had plenty of their own. We finally made a deal so that Joe Kirk got what he wanted but there wasn't any risk with King Ranch money if it didn't work out."

Several telephone conversations later, all of the parties involved agreed on a plan for King Ranch to take the stallion with an option to buy him until December 20. "The deal was that I'd train him and if we didn't want him, we could turn him back after the Futurity," continued Welch. "Structuring that trade right was important. We all agreed that we should not pay $50,000 for a green colt, so we had to figure out a way to structure the deal so everybody would be happy and there would be no big financial risk to the King Ranch."

At approximately 10:30 one night, about six weeks after Reeves returned from King Ranch, his telephone rang. Answering it, he heard his boss on the other end. "Joe Kirk Fulton told me, 'They're gonna be there in the morning to pick up that horse,' " remembered Reeves. "I asked, 'Which horse?' and when he told me Peppy San Badger, that Buster was going to train him for the futurity, my throat got kind of dry. That was a sad day. It really pained me to see him go, I'd gotten so attached to him. He'll always have a place in my heart."

Tio and Fulton signed the option to purchase Peppy San Badger for $50,000 plus 25 breedings to the horse spread over several years, on May 20, 1977. The King Ranch men felt the 25 breedings would enhance their program and were glad to be partners with Fulton, since they respected him as an astute horseman.

To King Ranch, Welch, with his expertise, was the man to best train the horse to his fullest potential. Trying to ease Reeves' distress of losing his futurity prospect, however, they furnished him with a horse to exhibit in the show and Welch continued to assist Reeves in gaining training experience.

"It was important to all of us that the relationship between Joe Kirk, Buster, Bruce, all of us, had to stay intact," explained Tio. "We could live without the horse, but not without the friendship. Our objective was to have this good-looking, young horse help us with our program, but not at the price of losing friends."

11

A NEW HOME

othing in this world can take the place of persistence. Talent will not; *nothing is more common than unsuccessful men with talent. Genius will not; unrewarded genius is almost a proverb. Education will not; the world is full of educated derelicts. Persistence and determination alone are omnipotent. The slogan "press on" has solved and always will solve the problems of the human race.*

Calvin Coolidge

It didn't take long for the majority of those associated with the Ranch, from barn help to King Ranch stockholders, to become infatuated with the stallion. Tio, however, was concerned about what his father's opinion of the new stallion might be. Peppy San Badger had white on him, a color King Ranch had shied away from with the horses on which Dick Kleberg had spent his life.

"It took him a while to become convinced the stallion was all right," stated Tio. "He was afraid that his offspring would have white feet and horses with white feet don't stand up in this country. We have sand and clay in the soil and a horse with white hair and pink skin underneath it would get sand burn.

"The clay on one of the Ranches gets like concrete; I could tell in his eyes when he first saw Peppy San Badger, he thought I had bargained for some problems. Peppy San Badger, however, had only streaks of white in his hooves and he never had any trouble with them. It didn't take Dad as long, though, to become impressed with him as the rest of us."

In an article on King Ranch in the September 1940, *The Cattleman*, Hazel Bowman explained further the reasoning behind "no white" and all sorrel horses on the Ranch:

> "At the outset, Mr. Kleberg was governed by climatic and physical conditions of the King Ranch territory in his choice as to the color of a horse which would be most practical for his purpose. In that section of Texas, horses are subject to an affliction known as sand burn, which is caused by some alkaline substance in the prairie sand and which blisters the hide of horses having any white patches on them. The all-sorrel was chosen by Mr. Kleberg because greys, duns and sorrels, with black skin, hold their color best in the heat and sun. After they shed in the spring, their coats do not sunburn. Furthermore, sorrel is the only recessive color. A sorrel, when bred to a sorrel, always produces the same color."

Life for Peppy San Badger dramatically changed with his new home. Rather than work in an arena and lope in the cotton fields as he had done with Reeves, Welch often carried his training stock to the pastures, believing the best lessons were born from every-day cattle works. Peppy San Badger, therefore, like the rest of the 3-year-olds, was loaded in a trailer and hauled to the cow camp site.

Pasture work, with clumps of grass, prickly pear, and now and then even a small offshoot of new mesquite scattering the land, differed from the dirt floor of the working arena, not only in physical surroundings but in its expectations from the horse as well. This was work in the real world, where a cutting horse separated a calf from a herd that could easily number 400, then held it at bay in the wide-open spaces until the cow wearied of trying to return to the herd.

As other cowboys ushered the cow to the herd of cut calves, the rider wheeled his horse around to separate another calf. With this kind of repetitious work, Peppy San Badger quickly learned the art of separating cow and calf and honed his instinctive 'cow sense' by holding one cow after another. Pasture work also quickly taught him the value of staying alert, else he might experience prickly pear, low stumps and a host of other earthly objects. Peppy San Badger adapted to the new challenges easily.

"I rode him a lot outside," stated Welch. "I worked calves at the roundup on him, roped 'em, and drug 'em to the fire. He was so smart, he'd figure out where the branding fire was and the shortest way to get there. He'd even turn and go under the rope if that was the shortest distance.

"Using horses like that on the Ranch takes away the monotony of a training program," he continued. "A horse seems to sense when you're doing something with a purpose and he learns from that. That was the way it was with Little Peppy. You don't see many cats get crippled catching mice. It's the same way with the horses. They're bred to do this and I seldom cripple a horse working him in natural surroundings."

With 60,000 head of cattle on King Ranch, work there was a dream world for Buster. "I really enjoyed working cattle horseback, so I had a lot of fun down there. I guess all the rest of it was a by-product of that. I'd gone down to King Ranch for a year, as a consultant, to sell Mr San Peppy and help get a horse program started. Joe, Tio and I made a great team to get that done. Then Little Peppy came along and he was such a magical horse; that even made it better."

MORE HELP NEEDED

While Welch polished on King Ranch's Quarter Horse program, the Ranch exploded with equine activity. Almost overnight, the number of young horses that needed breaking increased; yet there wasn't enough time to break them all. Welch's work with training the 2- and 3-year-olds resembled a merry go-round: dropping the reins of a sweaty mount he had just finished working into the hands of a cowboy, while sticking his boot into the stirrup of a fresh horse waiting its turn. He needed help and he found it during a summer circuit at Rex Cauble's ranch in Denton Texas. With Tio's approval, he hired cutting horse competitors Lank Creacy and Scott Overcash.

"Our first job was breakin' 60 head of broncs," remembered Creacy, "They had 'em in feed lots and me, Scott and another guy on the Ranch divided those colts up and went to work."

Creacy's job took him from the bronc pen, with fractious young colts, to the working arena, where he turned back for Welch, and then on to the seat of a truck, to haul horses to and from shows. Early one morning, in November 1977, he and Joe Stiles prepared for another trip. Creacy's trailer carried half of the colts that were bound for a preliminary Futurity work in Sweetwater, Texas.

Before climbing in the truck, he checked one more time to make sure water buckets had been loaded. He knew well the headache of arriving at a show in the middle of the night without enough water buckets; with seven horses to care for, he certainly did not want that to happen. Satisfied, he climbed behind the wheel and eased his rig onto the road behind Stiles who was pulling Ol' Blue, Buster's trailer with its rusting sides, also loaded with horses.

Creacy couldn't help but grin at the scene: Ol' Blue, showing its age with rust as its primary color, trailered along behind a shiny truck emblazoned with the words "1976 NCHA World Champion." In a way, though, it symbolized King Ranch: a mixture of old and new. Out on the highway, he checked his watch and then settled back for the 12-hour drive to Sweetwater. It would be a long time before his head hit a pillow.

SWEETWATER PREDICTIONS

Sweetwater pre-futurity practice was the "in" place to be prior to the NCHA Futurity. One of the trainers there was Joe Heim with his entry, Doc's Serendipity. Before the Futurity would end, Doc's Serendipty and Heim, who had apprenticed under Welch, would be a major threat to Peppy San Badger and Welch.

"In those days, that was the only organized practice, so probably 100 of the 300 horses that would show at the Futurity were there," relived Heim. "You pretty well knew by the way the practice went who your competition would be at the futurity."

Tio also attended the pre-work to scope Peppy San Badger's competition. "After watching the other horses that were there, I knew we had a good horse if we got him shown. Most of the serious competition came by way of Sweetwater for the practice on the way to the futurity, and some would "leave their Futurity" there, overworking their colts and taking the edge off of them. That certainly wasn't the case with Peppy San Badger. We really didn't know how good he was because Buster never asked him to do anything. His philosophy was, 'He's got what it takes to do the job and if I ask him, he'll respond.' "

Kleberg wasn't the only one impressed with Peppy San Badger. Helen Groves traveled to Texas for the Futurity and was also at the pre-works, liking what she both saw and felt. "I loped him for Buster while at Sweetwater," offered Helen Groves, "and that horse was totally ambidextrous. Most horses are left handed, but he was ambidextrous and a real thrill to ride.

"I had watched Buster work him earlier at the Ranch," she continued. "It was one of the few times he turned him loose and he was fantastic.

When he finished, I said, 'Buster, you'd better not do that again.' He asked me why I said that, and I told him, 'I'm afraid you'll rip the hind legs off of him!' It was the way he was using his hind legs, so powerful, that I feared for him."

Eighteen days prior to the NCHA Futurity, at the suggestion of Buster, King Ranch exercised its right to purchase the stallion. "I was pretty sure I had a chance to win the futurity," recalled Welch. "Of course, none of us ever know for sure, but I felt strongly enough about it that I was willing to say, 'Okay, the odds are good enough; he's worth buying to have in King Ranch's name should he win.' "

Peppy San Badger, affectionately known as "Little Peppy." Photo by Janell Kleberg.

Trainer Shorty Freeman had a similar intuition about the Futurity. He and Welch hosted the Sweetwater pre-works every year, helping others with their horses and swapping their own mounts with one another for evaluation while they were there. "Shorty worked Little Peppy for me a couple of times. That last time he worked him, he brought him back, handed him to me and said, 'Bus, I believe you're gonna win that Futurity.' "

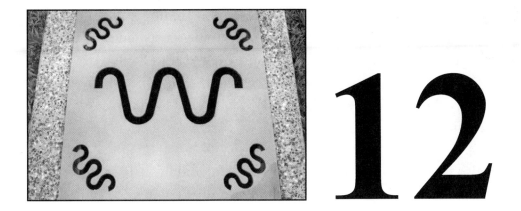

THE 1977 NCHA FUTURITY

S *teve Knudsen, loping Peppy San Badger in circles with other horses preparing to show in the evening performance, periodically glanced at the crowd flowing into the Will Rogers Coliseum seating area. He wasn't too sure, but maybe there were more people here than lived in Kingsville, Texas. Knudsen didn't know about how Welch felt, but all this excitement and all these people were nerve-wracking. Had it not been for Peppy San Badger making the Futurity finals, he'd just as soon been back on King Ranch where life was definitely more peaceful.*

About this time of evening, it'd be quiet on the Ranch, and if you sat real still under a mesquite, not even twitchin' a muscle, the night came alive around you. Crickets sang, coyotes yelped and dried grass and mesquite beans crunched under deer hooves or crawling creatures of the night.

Let your boot scoot just a hair on the sand, though, and it all became dead silence. Knudsen bet he could scoot both boots on the sand here in the arena and nobody would even notice. Glancing at the overflowing-crowd, he knew he was right, so he merely lowered his head again and kept loping, wondering where so many people came from, wondering if any of them had ever really known the sounds of night.

B arn 8, with its pungent odor of horse urine, hiding in the dirt from years of accumulation, along with the musty smell of the aging boards of its stalls, was home each year to the NCHA Futurity horses. In 1977, the stalls, which seemed to cling together, more by layers of sticky dust and cobwebs than nails, were about to house over 300 horses attending the show.

It was also home to the famed Stallion Row, the middle aisle of the barn where well-known stallions stood all week for public viewing, tolerating glaring lights, noisy crowds and poking fingers. Stallion owners, whether to disguise the barn or to help entice breeders to consider their wares, valiantly strived to create an esthetic appeal to Stallion Row. For King Ranch, it worked.

Several days before the Futurity kicked off, King Ranch employees scurried like ants around Barn 8, reconstructing a replica of the front of the famous King Ranch Carriage House, a familiar building even to those who had never visited the Ranch, since it was the backdrop in many King Ranch advertisements. Prior to traveling to Fort Worth, the prop had been built by King Ranch carpenters, who then tore it down to hauling-size pieces, loaded it on trucks and carried it to Fort Worth. Stretching across two separate aisles and four rows of stalls, the massive entry exhorted the majesty of King Ranch, permeating the air with a feel of old Texas grandeur.

"It was quite a display," said Knudsen. "The carpenters, Chon Utley and Evaristo Garza, had to go with us to rebuild it and it wasn't something you just stuck up there, either," he recalled, arms stretching out to emphasize its extensive size. "We went to Fort Worth about three days before the show started just to erect this thing and all of us worked hard the entire time to put it together before the show started."

The King Ranch exhibition was not only prestigious, it was also inviting. The courtly, social graces its people radiated, along with the warm, relaxed atmosphere pervading their area, pulled visitors like a magnet to the King Ranch exhibit. Even the stallions, their stalls attractively walled and spotlights shining on their glistening coats, seemed to understand they were hosts to the strangers milling around them.   Instead of hiding their heads in a corner, they spent much of their time curiously observing being observed. Their placement in the mock King Ranch carriage house made viewing them easy.

"When you stepped down our aisle, Mr San Peppy stood in the corner stall on the left," described Knudsen. "Next to him was a stall we used as a welcome center. It had a coffee machine and sales brochures and it separated Mr San Peppy from the other horses. On the other side of the aisle, across from Mr San Peppy, was Peppy San Badger, and the tack room separated Peppy San Badger from the remainder of the King Ranch horses."

While to the casual observer, the presentation was relaxed and enjoyable, behind the scenes, frantic work continued around the clock. The normal, everyday chores with horses - washing, grooming, feeding, loping, cleaning stalls - continued in Fort Worth, Texas, as they did in Kingsville. In addition, Ranch employees added other jobs, such as security guard and chauffeuring, to their long list.

"During those years, you couldn't leave the coliseum once you got in there," explained Buster. "With all that bunch of horses in there, it left the stalls kind of open to anybody, and back then, there were a few people who would sneak back there and do something to your horse. It just made you lay down and rest better knowing somebody was watchin' 'em."

A general feeling of uneasiness pervaded all of the competitors that year. For one reason, the purse stakes had steadily climbed higher since the inaugural Futurity. When Buster won the first Futurity in 1962 riding Money's Glo, he won $3,828.12. Fourteen years later, in 1976, at the previous year's Futurity, Olan Hightower, riding Colonel Freckles, had won $44,800.90, with the champion's earnings having grown a whopping $41,000. With the 1977 Futurity, the winner's take would even be larger, since more entries had flocked to compete in the event. Cutting had become serious business.

"People locked their tack stalls who had never locked them before," recalled Tio. "Joe and I, and the girls from the office, Mary Pennington and Susan Cude, took turns staying with our horses during the day. At night, someone slept in the tack room and there was a night watchman on duty as well."

While Kleberg and other Ranch employees manned the exhibition, Buster concentrated on his stallion. Concerned that Peppy San Badger might get too 'cow fresh' during his week in Fort Worth, he spent part of the days, when he wasn't showing, off the Will Rogers complex working and riding Peppy San Badger. Knudsen usually met Welch at the practice area with the stallion.

"I carried him out to Jim Milner's place, kind of across from the NCHA office at that time, for Buster to work him," said Knudsen. "If I was busy bathing or exercising another horse, one of the other boys would haul him for Buster, but I usually did it. Buster wouldn't do much; lope him mostly, then maybe work a cow or two on him and then I'd take him back to the coliseum and give him a bath."

Looking back on working the stallion, Buster, his eyes dancing at the retrospection, chuckled, "You know, I don't think he really needed it; I think I did all of that for me."

THE FUTURITY

Tio and his wife, Janell, accompanied by Joe Stiles, slowly elbowed their way through the thick, shoulder-to-shoulder crowd which poured over into the aisles in the Will Rogers Coliseum. Besides the overflow of people slowing their progress, hands constantly popped in front of Kleberg and Stiles to be shaken; one person after another momentarily detained them with praises on their stallion, asking about breeding to Mr San Peppy.

The very air seemed alive with enthusiasm, crackling like static electricity all over the big-domed building. Futurity excitement was like the flu; once it got started, almost everyone caught it.

The three, energized with the titillation of the evening performance, finally found the reserved box belonging to Welch and Agnew. Relieved to reach their seats, Tio inhaled a deep breath, trying to exhale anxiety as much as to breathe.

In an effort to relieve finals-night jitters, Kleberg slowly surveyed the remainder of the coliseum. Although, by then, King Ranch had its own reserved box, the view from this one was definitely better and tonight's performance demanded the best seat in the house. Observing the seats

Buster and Little Peppy, after their 1977 NCHA Futurity win, with (from left) Sheila Welch Joe Stiles and Tio Kleberg. Photo by Jerry Mills.

rapidly filling in every section, Kleberg nodded to himself. "Yes, this was the best seat in the house."

Immediately, memories of a Futurity only three years earlier flashed across his mind. He, Joe Stiles, and Bobby Shelton had come here to watch cutting horses. That was the same year that Uncle Bob had come to watch Helen's horse, Pay Twentyone, perform. Glancing upward, he scanned the coliseum seats until, finding the area in which they had sat, an irrepressible smile crossed his face. There, almost to the top they had sat; in the nose-bleed section as they called it. That memory encouraged other reflections on his fast-paced, roller-coaster ride with horses which had ultimately brought him to this box.

In the last three years, King Ranch horses, with the lease of Mr San Peppy and the inception of an outside breeding program, had moved them from behind their private wall into the public domain. It was a year ago last August, that King Ranch had sealed that lease with the stallion's purchase. Then, last March, this unique Mr San Peppy offspring, Peppy San Badger, stepped into their lives. Now, here he sat in the best seat in the house to watch a King Ranch stallion compete in the Futurity finals.

The first words of the Star Spangled Banner, officially opening the 1977 NCHA Futurity, brought Kleberg not only back from his reverie but to his feet as he quickly grabbed his Stetson from his head. . Then, following a flamboyant speech from the announcer, the Futurity was under way.

As the first horse to show slowly walked toward the herd, Tio scanned the back of the arena until he found Steve slowly loping Peppy San Badger. Deciding everything appeared in order, he turned his attention toward the herd of cattle; it was time to watch the cutting.

Buster was also attentively watching each horse work; his view, though, was from the arena floor. After several riders completed their run, Welch motioned Knudsen to bring Peppy San Badger to him. Attired for the occasion in a sport coat and scarf, Welch had come to the finals with winning on his mind and, therefore, dressed the part of the Champion of a prestigious event.

The horse designated to compete prior to Peppy San Badger in the finals was working as Welch tightened the girth strap on his saddle. The stallion was so alert and sensitive in his belly, Buster kept the flank cinch pulled close to the front. Then, with the agility that comes with performing a feat a hundred times a week, Welch lithely lifted himself onto the horse's back. He was ready, even anxious, for his turn to show.

Knudsen, now free from duty, walked to the fence stretching behind the judge's stand that separated show arena from loping area. It offered a a bird's eye view of the upcoming event.

Buster confidently believed that if everything went right, before the night was over, he'd add another Futurity belt buckle to his growing collection. Assurance, born from faith in his horse as well as himself, exuded from Welch. Looking around him, he could read on the faces of some of the other finalists, the anxiety that a showman often wears when he is uneasy about his horse performing well. Welch did not have that problem.

Peppy San Badger showed no signs of nervousness. The horse, which had calmly walked down concrete steps into a strange arena nine months earlier, displayed that same composure in the Will Rogers Coliseum, unruffled by other horses, the continuous commotion or the bright lights. Welch knew Little Peppy would do his part and if he cut good cattle for the stallion to work, they had an excellent chance of winning the Futurity.

Tio had watched Little Peppy work every cow since the first go-round, had seen every particle of sand his hooves tossed into the air and had witnessed every flicker of his ears. His runs in the two go-rounds and finals were etched into his mind. Now, with his eyes riveted once again on Little Peppy, Kleberg suddenly felt this would be the run that would wipe all others from his mind.

The only nagging detriment to the evening was the stallion's draw, early in the first bunch of cattle. Each time Tio considered it, the thought hovered dark clouds over his expectations. It was commonly considered in the cutting horse world that those horses who worked later in the Futurity had the better draw since judging had a tendency to get looser as the evening progressed.

Kleberg also knew that while every entry was a threat, at least one serious contender for the Futurity crown drew late in the finals. Doc's Serendipity, a mare owned by David Brown of Eden Prairie, Minnesota, and shown by Joe Heim, had given phenomenal performances throughout the week.

A new, five-judge system replacing the previous three-judge system; however, had been inaugurated by NCHA at this event. It allowed the highest and the lowest judges' scores to be thrown out, then the three judges' scores remaining were added together for the accumulative score. Judges for the event were Tommy Moore, Ft Worth, Texas; Les Fuller, Dallas, Texas; James Kenny, Carlsbad, New Mexico; Jack Rydberg, Wiley, Colorado and Norman Bruce, Grayson, Georgia. Kleberg hoped the new system worked to his favor.

It seemed the Futurity had barely gotten under way when the spokesman announced, "The next horse to work is Peppy San Badger, owned by King Ranch and ridden by Buster Welch!"

As on cue, Buster, who had moved from behind the loping area to wait beside the judges' stands, confidently signaled Little Peppy to start the show. Obediently, the stallion, ears forward, eyes locking on the cattle, moved stealthily toward the waiting herd. Rather than disturbing the cattle, Little Peppy's soft approach let him glide though the herd, parting the cattle evenly down the middle, as Moses had once parted the Red Sea. Silence settled over the arena. The crowd, who had witnessed the stallion's previous runs, became deathly quiet in anticipation.

With the expertise of a professional, Little Peppy adeptly turned back toward the judges' stands, pushing the cattle in front of him, now with a sense of urgency. Unobtrusively, following the guiding language from his master, he focused on an unsuspecting cow, inching her away from the herd farther and farther until she stood as in exile, in the middle of the pen. The performance had been an exercise in ballet.

Immediately, however, as the cow, realizing its dilemma, dived toward the security of the herd, Little Peppy ripped aside his demur disposition and exploded into fiery motion. Head low, front legs sprawled in defense, he challenged again and again the daring attempts of the cow. The crowd, at his first splatter of defiance, boisterously bellowed their approval.

"I had never seen a horse work like that before," marveled Helen Groves. "He almost galloped out to the middle of the pen, pushing that cow he cut in front of him, and then he worked her, never allowing her to push him back, but never driving forward either. No one drives out like that anymore. I've seen some good runs, but this one was special and the reaction from the crowd was tremendous."

Little Peppy worked like no other horse the crowd had ever witnessed and they loved it. Quick and snappy, he reeled himself from side to side, stopping the calf's encounter in midstream, foiling another encounter before it started, reading her movements almost before she made them. Just as quickly as he attacked on one side, he was back, planting his body in her face, his head low, legs stretched in a stance of defiance. As the crowd still thundered its approval, Welch signaled the stallion to stop and returned once more to the herd.

Seasoned with years of cattle knowledge, Welch once again picked an excellent species for Little Peppy to work. a bold self assurance encircled both him and the stallion as they went deep into the herd to again push free a second cow without even a hint of hesitation. Among the brush land of King Ranch, Little Peppy had practiced this art time and again, and now it paid off in big bucks.

To the stallion, the night's performance of ceaseless suspense-filled action was merely a game. When the buzzer finally sounded the end of his 2 ½ minute run, the noise of the crowd reverberated from side to side as a score of 220.5 flashed on the score board.

"That brought the house down and that run probably changed the style of cutting," affirmed Joe Stiles. "Up until that point, most everyone had horses running and stopping real flat. This horse faced up to a cow more than was popular at the time. He faced up, sat down like a cat, and drew back. The next year, everybody came to the Futurity with a changed way of cutting."

Sam Shepard, a cutting horse trainer and later NCHA President, agreed. "He was an amazing animal. He reminded me of a great big leopard, the way he moved. He would just leap through the air from one side to another. It was very unorthodox for a cutting horse" (*Cutting Horse Chatter*, Feb 1993, p. 22)

Wayne Pooley was also impressed with the run. "To me, he was set apart; he was so cowy and every move he made at that finals was made with an authority and quickness. The only reason he was there was to cut. He wasn't worried about the crowd or another horse; this horse was there to show the crowd what he could do, and he had them hollering."

Knudsen, grinning from one ear to ear, stood in Buster's path as he rode behind the judges' stand, breathing easier now that the run was over. Welch, his own smile lighting up his face, stepped from Little Peppy and handed Knudsen the reins as Joe Heim, a main competitor still to show, walked over to them and shook Buster's hand. Heim had one time worked for Welch and now, without splint boots in which to show Doc's Serendipity, he had come to borrow Little Peppy's.

"I didn't have any splint boots to show in," recalled Heim, "so as soon as Buster finished his run, we took them off of Little Peppy and I put them on Doc's Serendipity."

Characteristic of the sport of cutting, men who competed fiercely against one another when showing their horses for 2 ½ minutes, also helped their competitor when it came their time to show. They shared equipment, turned back in the arena for one another and even offered advice. Even though Welch hoped he had just won the most prestigious cutting event, he attended to the needs of his friend.

"Buster got marked," remarked Knudsen, "but we all knew we had to wait out Joe's run. He worked late in the show and until he cut, no one came close to Buster's score."

Welch watched intently as Heim rode his mare to the herd. He knew he was watching a good hand sitting on the back of a good horse.

"I thought I had a good run," remembered Joe. "I cut my turn back help. When that happened, I had to turn around quickly and just peel a cow from the herd. We scored a 220, ½ point behind Buster."

Little Peppy had won the coveted 1977 NCHA Futurity while Doc's Serendipity was Reserve champion. The same pair of splint boots had protected the legs of both the horses. Now the famed King Ranch owned not only a two-time NCHA World Champion, but also an NCHA Futurity Champion. The fact that the stallions were sire and son was icing on the cake.

13

CHANGES AT KING RANCH

I f gravity is the glue that holds the universe together, balance is the key that unlocks its secrets. Balance applies to our body, mind, and emotions, to all levels of our being. It reminds us that anything we do, we can overdo or under do, and that if the pendulum of our lives or habits swings too far to one side, it will inevitably swing to the other."

The Laws of Spirit, by Dan Millman; H.J.Kramerr, Publisher Tiburon, California, 1995. P.8.

In her office at King Ranch, Mary Pennington had hardly hung up the telephone before another insistent shrill demanded attention. The calls were preambles to the 1978 breeding season, which was

113

bearing down on King Ranch like a runaway locomotive.

Its stallion, Mr San Peppy, already boasting a glowing list of credentials, now added to that list was the claim of having sired the 1977 NCHA Futurity Champion. As an addendum, the Futurity Champ, Peppy San Badger resided there also. Wagering mare owners believed the stallions were glowing embers, ready to burst like flames on the industry and fan its future. The inflow of mail corroborated the bet: Peppy was a hot item and his son, a close second. Daily, as the postman made his rounds, a new stack of envelopes awaited him, filled with contracts for potential breeders who were anxious to "sign on the dotted line." Daily, he also returned to King Ranch with another stack of envelopes which contained signed contracts.

ACCOLADES FOR MR SAN PEPPY

With Little Peppy being a product of the first crop of colts by Mr San Peppy, Kleberg and Welch envisioned a new crop every year with equally exceptional talents. Owners of some of the most desired mares encouraged that vision by rushing to book breedings to Mr San Peppy. Surely, Little Peppy's sire, whose court quickly filled with one proven producer after another, would sire more offspring as good as, and hopefully even better than, Little Peppy.

Although winning the Futurity was a momentous occasion, King Ranch embraced the achievement more as an assurance for Mr San Peppy's ability to sire outstanding foals rather than an accolade along Little Peppy's road to stardom. The purpose of buying Mr San Peppy was to own a producing sire and Little Peppy proved they did. Since they set a course several years earlier to use the offspring's accomplishments as stepping stones to promote the stallion, King Ranch felt Little Peppy was merely a first in a long line of successful progeny. To King Ranch, their program was right on course.

*Buster Welch riding Mr San Peppy in a herd of
Santa Gertrudis on King Ranch.*

*Sea of cattle at
King Ranch.*

Buster Welch riding Peppy San Badger
at the Norias Division of King Ranch.

Peppy San Badger.

Breeding facilities at King Ranch.

*Mares and foals in the pasture
at King Ranch.*

*La Le, who worked
for King Ranch
for many years.*

Yearlings at
King Ranch.

Photos courtesy King Ranch Archives, King Ranch, Inc.

Photo by Janell Kleberg.

Roberto Silguero (Beto) with a herd of steers at King Ranch.

Photo courtesy King Ranch Archives,
King Ranch, Inc.

A King Ranch vaqueros saddle and blanket.

120

A saddle on a windmill pipe at cow camp.

Mares and foals at sunset on King Ranch.

Many top sales were held at King Ranch over the years. Gary Don Hopkins leads horses to the sale ring. (Left) Joe Stiles and Tio Kleberg going over pedigrees at a sale. (Right) Tio and Scott Kleberg.

A NEW OWNER

Buster knew King Ranch wanted him to continue showing Mr San Peppy, but, like other trainers, he was eager to test the waters of the week-end competition with his Futurity winner.

"I wanted to take Little Peppy on the road," said Buster. "With them just breaking into the business and still a little unsure about the showing, taking a chance on two horses paying their way going down the road, was a little much to ask. We were working to keep the Ranch program economically feasible, so after winning the Futurity, I approached Tio about letting me buy Little Peppy, with King Ranch holding an option to buy him back. At that time, we thought we would get another 100 horses like Little Peppy sired by Mr San Peppy. We didn't realize that Little Peppy was a unique colt sired by Mr San Peppy, not the normal colt."

Welch took over the ownership of Little Peppy on December 28, 1977, and began the year alternating the horses in open competition. Sheila, at the same time, won check after check on Little Peppy in the non-pro class, even winning the prestigious Houston Livestock Show and Rodeo Non-Professional class. By the end of March, she and Little Peppy led the NCHA Non-Professional standings with $6,003.44. Buster had both of the stallions in the NCHA standings. Mr San Peppy was sitting 6th in the NCHA Standings with earnings of $4,104.23 while Little Peppy was 12th, having won $1,826.24.

FIRST $100,000 WINNER

Early in the year, Zack Wood, Executive Director of the National Cutting Horse Association, while updating records, realized Mr San Peppy had almost won $100,000, a phenomenal feat for a horse at that time. The records showed that Mr San Peppy had earnings of $95,832.73 in Open competition alone, excluding his 1972 NCHA Derby check. There had never been a horse to break the $100,000 earnings mark in Open competition, so Wood shared the information with Welch.

"After Zack told me there'd never been a horse to do that and Peppy was that close, I decided to try to get that 'first' for his record," said Buster. "We still thought he was 'the sire' for the breeding program. I began only showing Peppy until I got it done."

The men of King Ranch often took turns hauling Mr San Peppy, but for the stallion to accumulate over $95,000, it had literally been a long, hard road for the horse. It meant standing lengthy hours in a trailer, mile after mile, with the hot sun heating the metal that surrounded him in the summer, and freezing weather with icicles hanging from it in the winter. It meant loping, sometimes in easy sand, sometimes on ground as hard as concrete with small, menacing rocks lurking underneath, threatening harm to a hoof. It meant cutting good cattle, bad cattle and even wild cattle.

Welch meticulously kept a record of Peppy's growing accumulated earnings, looking for the show in which the stallion would set another milestone. It happened in Waco, Texas, and later, the cover of the October 1978 *Cutting Hoss Chatter* pictured Mr San Peppy and Welch with the caption, "First Winner of over $100,000 in open cutting!"

"I can just see that day!" said Welch. "It was a $200-added cutting when he went over the line," remembered Welch. "I believe it was the best run he ever had. He seemed to know this one could do it so he laid down a heck of a run."

1978 DERBY

Both stallions, stacking one winning run on top of another, fueled the conversation of cutting-horse people from coast to coast. To accomplish Mr San Peppy's milestone, and to keep Little Peppy high in the NCHA standings, the King Ranch trailer continually rolled down the highway, traveling from one show to another. However, now that trailer was a shiny, six-horse trailer. Steve Knudsen, Joe Stiles and others hauled the stallions.

Welch especially remembered one of those hauls. "It was about 3:00 a.m. when the phone rang," he remembered. "I just didn't want to wake up and answer it, but finally I reached over and picked it up. Robert McKay from Australia was hauling the horses to California for us at the time and it was Robert on the line. He said, 'Buster, the studs come off the trailer.' I jumped out of that bed, wide awake, a picture goin' through my mind of him scraping the top of the trailer, somehow, and just horses laying everywhere!

"By that time, I'm standing in the middle of the bedroom and I said, 'Well, what happened, Robert?' He answered, 'I don't know. The wheel just come running by me; all the studs come off that wheel!' "

The four-day NCHA Derby, an up-and-coming aged event for 4-year-old horses, had changed its name since the days when Mr San Peppy won the event six years earlier. When the event was called the "Maturity," the horse had pocketed slightly over $3,000. The show continued to gain notable prestige, and by 1978, during Little Peppy's 4-year-old year, 110 horses came to vie for the Derby Championship. He was one of them.

Even though Little Peppy was now owned by Welch, King Ranch, viewing him as a potential advertisement for Mr San Peppy and remained highly interested in his successes. "I had a great deal of confidence in the horse winning the Derby if Buster could get the cattle cut for him," remembered Tio. "At that time, we knew what we had in the horse. The concern with a mediocre horse was getting him shown; with a great horse like Little Peppy, it was, 'Could we show him.' "

Buster could show him.

This time, Little Peppy swept the Finals with a score of 219, leading his closest contender by 2.5 points. Besides becoming the 1978 NCHA Derby Champion, he also set a record as being the first Derby Champion to be sired by an NCHA Derby Champion.

In one last unusual feat, both sire and son ended the year in the NCHA

Top 10 Standings. Mr. San Peppy, having won $11,531.04, sat in 8th place, while Peppy San Badger, with earnings of $9,479.18, sat in 10th place. Had all the earnings been won by only one horse, that stallion would have been in 4th place at the end of the year.

PURCHASING A STALLION

For King Ranch, it was a year of reevaluation. Although Mr San Peppy remained a hot prospect in the breeding market, having 172 foals registered to him in 1979, resulting from the 1978 breeding year, the desire of mare owners to breed to his son, Peppy San Badger, grew just as demanding.

"We didn't expect that," admitted Tio. "We thought Mr San Peppy would draw all the interest since he had sired Little Peppy. The cutting industry; however, saw potential in the offspring as well as the sire and interest exploded in breeding to Little Peppy."

The reasons, perhaps, were many. The stallion's stunning Futurity performance had shaken an industry already experiencing change initiated in the early 70's by the offspring of Doc Bar. With Little Peppy's addition of fluid movements, coated with a new face-the-cow style, he performed professional work with an artistic flair, a kind of symphony with a cow and he conducted the show. It contrasted vividly from the earlier brusque-moving, rougher-textured cow horses, including Mr San Peppy, which the cutting community was accustomed to. Like styles changing in cars, the pendulum was swinging from the strong-moving, rugged sire to the finesse and charisma of his son.

The changing trend; however, was only one reason why interest was swinging toward Little Peppy. Contrary to previous visions, none of the 1975 colt crop sired by Mr San Peppy, which, by 1978, was in training, exuded the pizzazz and vigor of Little Peppy. Even though Mr San Peppy was a two-time World champion, the titles were fast becoming anticlimatic behind the growing prestige of aged events and Little Peppy's Futurity and Derby Championships.

126

Dr. John Toelkes, veterinarian for King Ranch, still offered another possibility for the change in interest. "The young horse overshadowed the old horse early on. The magic wasn't there with Mr San Peppy as it was with Little Peppy. Some of it may have been athletic ability but I think a lot of it was just cosmetic. The young horse was bigger and more eye appealing. I also think standing them both here together helped Little Peppy take mares away from the old man, but we didn't know that at the time. Mr San Peppy just became a faded glory behind him."

As Little Peppy's popularity continued to grow, Kleberg recalled, once more, the wisdom of his father, Dick Kleberg, when the younger Kleberg had believed that getting a good colt only required breeding a good mare to a good stallion. The elder Kleberg's words pierced his thoughts: "Trying to find a good stud is hard; trying to raise one is harder and raising a damned good one is near impossible!"

Dr. John Toelkes. Photo courtesy of King Ranch Archives, King Ranch, Inc..

With the words echoing in his mind, Kleberg realized they had their good stud and the odds of having another one year after year were slim. Tio sat down with Welch to discuss King Ranch's option of taking Little Peppy back at the end of the year.

COURTING A NEW VET

Dr. Jerry Morrow, the full-time veterinarian of King Ranch needed help. The cattle business alone swamped him with duties and now the equine business had mushroomed. There weren't enough hours in the day to professionally handle both programs; so daily, depending on whether the horses or the cattle demanded the most attention, the other one rated second-best care. Kleberg searched for an assistant to help Dr. Morrow. The search escalated when Dr. Morrow left the Ranch in the spring of 1978. Welch remembered a proficient horseman who was in a veterinary practice in Abilene, Texas, having just relocated there from Oklahoma.

"I remembered these two veterinarians working a bunch of wild mares for me at Charlie Boyd's place," said Buster. "They impressed me with their work because that wasn't an easy job. Down at King Ranch, we needed to work with good people, people you wanted to be around because we were all so closely involved with each other. I thought John Toelkes might fit in real well, so I recommended him to Tio."

Late one September afternoon in 1978, veterinarian John Toelkes wound down his work day. Buster, whom Toelkes knew, but with whom he had not talked in several years, called to offer him a job.

"I didn't even think about it. I immediately said no," remembered Toelkes. "I'd never even considered leaving Abilene. We'd been living there since 1975 and although I had a little 'burn out' with my vet practice, we liked the town and had good friends there and our children liked their schools. I couldn't see any reason to move."

Buster, however, being the persuasive negotiator, still invited John to bring his wife, Jamene, and come visit the Ranch for a weekend. That idea appealed to Toelkes.

"I was in a little trouble with my wife, having been gone for almost a month with several clients. It wasn't that I'd been gone so long," stated John, "but the fact that I'd gone to France and she had to stay home, now that upset her. I decided this trip might help appease Jamene."

The visit, while appeasing Jamene, impressed him as well. King Ranch rolled out the red carpet for the Toelkeses, entertaining them with the history of the famous land, sharing the traditional family atmosphere where employees still ate breakfast and lunch at the Ranch and introducing them to the *Kinenos*, the good people who helped get every job accomplished on King Ranch. After 16 years of a mixed-animal practice, the idea of working only with horses and concentrating on a new breeding program stirred in Toelkes an old interest of his Oklahoma days.

Several years after Welch and Toelkes had first become acquainted in Abilene, Toelkes had been in an active broodmare practice in Norman, Oklahoma, the center of the running Quarter Horse world, where artificial insemination was heavily practiced. Welch stopped by one of the breeding farms to visit one day.

"Buster and Jay Agnew walked in on us in the spring of 1973 while we were breeding in Oklahoma," remembered Toelkes. "They looked the place over, we visited a little bit, and then they were gone. A couple of years later, we moved back to Abilene."

King Ranch life did not mirror the hectic schedule of the mixed animal practice in a town the size of Abilene with its population of 110,000. Almost on the opposite side of Texas, removed from heavy population, industrial pollution, and the frenzy of the modern day world, the relaxed atmosphere surrounding King Ranch appealed to both of the Toelkeses.

"There was quite a little courtship between us for the next several weeks," said Toelkes. "I finally asked Tio one morning, 'We breed for only five or six months out of the year; then what do I do?' He answered, 'Whatever you want to do.' "

Toelkes ruefully admitted, "That probably cinched the deal." Then, with a smile and a slow shake of his head at the memory, he added, "But somehow, it's never worked that way."

The Toelkeses discussed the opportunity with their children, who agreed to a new challenge. In January 1979, with stacks of marked boxes identifying possessions from dishes to veterinary books, the family moved to Kingsville, Texas.

THE INITIATION YEAR

By culling and grading mares the year before, King Ranch had a full roster of its own mares to breed. In addition, with its reputation rapidly spreading as an exceptional commercial breeding operation, trailers daily rolled into the Ranch from February to May, checking in mares. By 1979, Mr San Peppy stood to the public for $2,500, while Little Peppy, whose breeding fee in 1978 was $1250, had now also risen to $2500.

"We had 350 of our own mares to breed when I came here," stated Toelkes, relating his first year on the job. "We collected Mr San Peppy and Little Peppy to artificially inseminate their mares and pasture bred four other stallions: Doc Holiday, El Rey Rojo, El Pobre and El Aguado."

With sufficient barn and pasture space, outside mares stayed at the Mare Barn and in paddocks surrounding it, an area just up from headquarters. Ranch mares were kept at a separate location across the Santa Gertrudis Creek from the Main House, referred to by employees as the "Creek Barn." Keeping track of King Ranch's own mares to be bred to the stallions posed more of a problem than keeping track of the outside mares.

In previous years, King Ranch had developed an identification method, including several brands. On the left butt, they branded the symbol for the sire and on the left thigh, they branded the famous Running W Ranch brand. On the right butt was the brand of the maternal sire while a number brand was placed on the right side of the neck of the fillies. Both fillies and colts were lip tattooed with a number. Since most King Ranch mares were solid sorrel and line breeding had marked them with similar characteristics, often making full sisters pass for identical twins, their brands offered the only guarantees of their parentage, but not their age. Unfortunately, the fire brands placed on many of the older mares had faded. Toelkes searched for an alternative to the identification process.

"In other places I had worked, we used collars to identify the mares, so we tried that, but pretty quickly the collars were falling off," recalled Toelkes. "Our mares were all kept in pastures and one mare would start grooming on another mare, soon having her collar loose. Those ends on the plastic collars attracted the mares and they'd nibble on them and loosen them.

"To keep the collars on, we decided to tape the ends together, and then someone got the idea to use colored tape to identify which mare was to be bred to which horse. That way, you could look down a line of mares that you were going to inseminate and the tape should show all of one color: either blue, red or green. Blue tape represented Little Peppy, red tape represented Mr San Peppy and green tape referred to other stallions in the A.I. unit to which mares were to be bred.

NATURE'S GREETING

Toelkes had finally settled into the routine at King Ranch, working out many of the kinks of an unplanned rush on the commercial breeding program and was feeling rather comfortable with making such a major move when, suddenly, Mother Nature brought her greetings.

"In early August 1980, we had the sale colts up, getting them fitted and ready for the upcoming yearling sale," reminisced Steve Knudsen. "The weather started getting bad with a hurricane out in the Gulf; then the next thing we know, Hurricane Allen is headed straight toward us."

Horses meant responsibilities, and since there were too many to move, Toelkes felt he needed to stay and weather out the storm. "We were somewhat anxious about our first hurricane." remembered Toelkes. "We had some summer visitors, two boys the same age as our kids, and, of course, Jamene was apprehensive about the kids. I decided that we would just all weather the storm out at the Ranch. The vet supply room at the Ranch was all concrete and brick with few windows, kind of like a bomb shelter, so it was a good place to stay. If the storm was really bad, we had fresh water at the lake and the Commissary was still functional, so we had plenty to eat."

Knudsen and his family, which included 13-month-old Leslie, born in July, joined the Toelkes to wait out Hurricane Allen. Although the hurricane hesitated a day before hitting King Ranch, the roaring winds and pounding rains pummeled headquarters when it arrived.

"The wind blew so strong that the bump gate stood wide open," remembered Steve, "and big limbs, salt cedars, the big window shades and all kinds of stuff came rolling down the road right in front of us.

"What was most amazing to me, was to watch the horses during that storm," added Toelkes. "They just stood there with their butt to it and took it. The wind was howling and the rain pouring down with lots of force against them, so I know they were tired when it was all over."

Several of the younger workers remained also, staying in the barn with the resident horses while 110-mile-per-hour winds blew through the Ranch. After Knudsen felt that the major impact had passed, he stepped out the back door of the the Vet Office to run for the barn behind it and check on the young workers. About that time, a portion of the roof ripped away from the barn, flying like a missile across the yard.

"That scared me," remembered Steve. "It had taken two or three guys to lift that heavy sheet up on that roof when they had built it, and the wind rolled it across that roof and then threw it into the air like it was a piece of tin."

Knudsen bolted for the barn and found the young workers, frightened but unscathed, at its far end, where a gaping hole now appeared in the area that had one time covered Mr San Peppy's stall. The stallion, unharmed, stood quietly in a corner while pelting rains flooded his stall.

"We were fortunate, though," added Knudsen. "None of the people got hurt, none of the animals got hurt and we really only had minor structural damage. It could have been a lot worse."

Mother Nature, as she often did with droughts, had once again reminded those living at King Ranch, that she, indeed was boss.

14

A HECTIC SCHEDULE

S mashing out his cigarette with one hand, while deftly turning his Buick toward the arena with the other, Dick Kleberg jammed on the brakes just before the nose of his car plowed into the fence. Although on oxygen all of the time now, he still adamantly smoked his cigarettes and these days drove his own car. He had dismissed his compadre, Javiel Quintanilla, sometime back, wanting the freedom of being alone. On the Ranch, with its hardships and vast spread, the two always traveled together. While they were boss and employee, they were also companions, friends whose lives could intertwine closer than brother's. Still, these days, he preferred to be alone to do as he pleased, when he chose and without someone telling him he shouldn't be smoking while on oxygen.

Kleberg's eyes darted around the arena until they fastened on Buster Welch, sitting motionless on the back of Peppy San Badger. Unconsciously, he slightly nodded his head with satisfaction. Buster was a good horseman; just like a fly, still and quiet one minute, moving like lightning the next.

Little Peppy, unmindful of his rider, played with the cow, ears forward, his legs in perpetual motion. Kleberg liked that horse; in fact, the thought of watching the young stallion work helped get him out of bed these mornings. With his failing health, there had to be some reason to put forth that effort.

As Kleberg watched, his mind drifted to his own years of working cattle. The back of a horse had always been comfortable to him, his security zone, whether just riding through the herd or in the heat of battle. Mentally, he saw himself and his horse time and again pitted against nature and a wild cow; racing headlong, rope whipping above his head, mindful of gopher holes but refusing to relent to them. The surge of satisfaction that never dulled from working with a good animal felt as good in his memory as it had then. He and Uncle Bob had worked hard to carry on King Ranch's reputation of outstanding livestock. He wished Uncle Bob were here today to see this horse.

Smiling to himself, he wondered what Bob Kleberg would say about the "chrome" on Peppy San Badger. Heck, you couldn't have convinced him 20 years ago, let alone Bob Kleberg, that King Ranch would own a horse with white on him. He had to admit, though, this horse was unique all the way around.

Welch, dismounting from Peppy San Badger, returned Kleberg from his reverie with yesterday to the present. Immediately, he began honking his horn, gaining Buster's attention, waving his hand to motion for him to come over. Buster handed the reins of Little Peppy to an employee and quickly strode over to the Buick. He liked Mr Dick. He had always been a cowman and a horseman and those were Buster's favorite people.

"Mornin' Mr. Dick," said Buster, bending down to peer in the driver's side window at the patriarch of King Ranch.

Without any acknowledgment, but with deep furrows embedded between his eyebrows, Kleberg gruffly answered, "Buster, I'm mad at you!"

Somewhat taken back by the statement, Buster looked a little closer at the ailing gentleman who was still fiercely in control of his independence. "Well, what have I done, Mr. Dick," he asked, his mind rolling in search of a misdeed he might have committed to upset the boss.

Kleberg's expression immediately turned from gruff and menacing to pleased, having one more time pulled an unsuspecting prank. "You're gettin' to ride that horse and I can't!"

Buster smiled at the old gentleman as well as at the irony of the statement.

Kleberg, the epitome of a good horseman who roped, branded and worked cattle all his life, had lived Welch's dream. Now Buster, on the back of Little Peppy, was living a dream of Kleberg's. Life was full of little ironies.

"Things like Little Peppy don't just happen," reminisced Buster. "It takes a dream team to make it happen. It takes people following one after another, like Jay Agnew, a horseman and a driving force behind Peppy; Wayne Pooley, who was really a good horseman and recognized Peppy's talent; Joe Kirk Fulton, who was a connoisseur of horses, and King Ranch, who promoted him. It's a process through time. All those people are the reasons Little Peppy happened."

There were others, in addition to the men who were stepping stones in the creation and promotion of Little Peppy. They, however, were usually behind the scenes, taking care of his daily routine.

At 6:00 every morning, Steve Knudsen, Scott Overcash and Lank Creacy, along with seasoned *vaqueros* and young 'wannabe'

Steve Knudsen. Photo courtesy of King Ranch Archives, King Ranch, Inc.

cowboys, gathered at the cook house on one end of headquarters for breakfast before beginning the day. At that time, King Ranch fed its employees both breakfast and lunch, a long-standing tradition, with them spending from daylight-to-dark days out on the range.

By 7:00 a.m., the men were horseback, racing against time to get horses loped and worked before the afternoon sun made loping too unbearably hot. Morning temperatures, usually staying in the upper 80's or low 90 degrees and, heavy with humidity, were more bearable than the stifling early afternoons when heat, thickly settling in the air, seemed powerful enough to suffocate both man and beast. Sometimes, though, on the more fortunate days, breezes softened the crushing effects of the heat. Those who lived on the Ranch adjusted, their body temperatures accommodating the environment.

"I spent most of my time either in the pen turning back for Buster, loping horses around that track or hauling them to shows," remembered Creacy. "I loped many a mile around that old track behind the Race Horse Barn where they use to train Thoroughbreds. Every day Buster was away from the Ranch, I loped both Little Peppy and Peppy. Me, Scotty and Steve just kept a steady stream of horses going around the track."

1980: HAULING FOR ANOTHER WORLD TITLE

Even though Little Peppy's credentials pleased his loyal followers, Welch wanted one more title for the stallion. Welch wanted to make Little Peppy a World Champion Cutting Horse like his sire and set out in 1979 to do so, knowing that he was so eye appealing, he would attract people and thus attract breeders.

"Little Peppy had an intangible quality that drew people," reminisced Janell Kleberg. "It was an equine charisma that is hard to describe. He was sensitive to the humanity around him, a gentle spirit with a tremendous heart."

During the early part of the year, when mares and breeding demands were still months away, Welch, a seasoned veteran of hauling horses for World championship titles, loaded Little Peppy in the trailer and hit the show road. Competitors in Texas followed a similar route, kicking off the year in Midland, then attending eight days of shows at the Arizona Sun

136

Country Circuit in Maricopa, Arizona. At those shows, by laying down one remarkable run after another and winning his share of the shows with them, Little Peppy immediately became the topic of whispered conversation among the cutting crowd.

Placing in six of the Sun Circuit's eight shows, never lower than 2nd, the accomplishments netted him $3400; plenty of earning to set him off and running toward the laurels of a World Champion. The next stop was four days of showing at the 2nd annual Sun 'N Fun Cutting Circuit held in Las Vegas, Nevada, where he once again racked up earnings.

"Little Peppy was workin' like a house afire," remembered Welch. "He was just on target and we were winnin' every one of those suckers we could get to."

After padding their pockets with dollars from cuttings west of Texas, Welch returned to the Texas stock shows where the stallion won the San Antonio Livestock Exposition with an accumulative score of 451, a scorching five points ahead of second place. Following the San Antonio show, King Ranch, who had joined the list of circuit hosts, held three days of shows February 17-19. Rather than compete, however, Little Peppy munched hay in his stall while King Ranch people entertained the guests.

A FIRST CLASS SHOW

"We put the show on for our customers and since I worked those cattle all of the time, we felt I'd have an advantage, so I didn't show," explained Welch of his absenteeism from the entries. "Everybody wanted to see King Ranch, so the Ranch, itself, was a great calling card. The cuttings were more than just a show, though, they were a 'happening'. People came to watch who could afford to buy good cutting horses and because of those shows, they got into the business. We put on demonstrations with our horses and we showed them the mares and colts as well, but the emphasis was on showing, and everybody having a good time."

King Ranch cuttings were definitely the event to attend. It was three days of royal treatment in a festive atmosphere. As the cutters arrived, *Kinenos*, stationed at the entrance, in the barn and at the arenas, became welcoming crews, courteously directed the cowboys in parking their rigs, helping them find stalls in which to put their horses, answering questions and giving directions. Not only did the Ranch play the perfect host, it offered glimpses of another life that most competitors had never seen.

King Ranch showed Little Peppy at cutting so that the public could see him work, as well as give him the opportunity to win the NCHA World Championship. Buster is shown here with Little Peppy. Photo by Louise L. Serpa, courtesy of Sheila Welch.

"It was just a fun show to go to, so different than all the others," remembered Sharon Riddle, a non-pro competitor and wife of trainer Terry Riddle. "We went on helicopter rides and saw how they used them to herd the cattle. King Ranch was also one of the first events to offer separate classes in which just the ladies cut."

Besides witnessing the latest method of cattle gathering, visitors also witnessed the thrill of *vaqueros* bringing up a band of broodmares. Those more observant first noticed in the far distance a barely distinguishable haze hovering in the air. Before long, the haze turned to clouds of dust boiling from the ground, the result of thundering hooves pounding toward the arena as hundreds of mares, all sorrel, interwove their variations of brown against the backdrop of dust-filled air and khaki-colored ground. Their arrival to the pens surrounding the cutting arena, a majestic impressive sight reminiscent of movie scenes, always stopped the cutting.

In addition, the cattle used for the show created an intense competition of their own. Brash and brazen, they determinedly resisted the horses who had come to hold them, making those horses, who could tolerate their pressure, give gritty, often wild and reckless, performances. For those who made a run, the scores ran high.

Large pots of coffee and breakfast taquitos cooked by *Kinenos* adjacent to the covered arena kick-started the day for the cutters. Then at noon, they returned for lunch, the proceeds from the meals always benefiting a local charity.

"The aroma sifting up into the bleachers while they cooked lunch was mouth-watering," reminisced Gay Freeman Fosberg, the wife of the late Shorty Freeman. "I remember wonderful beef and a pita (camp) bread that they handed you hot off the grill. At that time, we lived in Arizona and going to the King Ranch cuttings was like a going to a big party and family reunion, all rolled up in one. We always felt so welcomed there."

Later in the evening, after all the horses were bathed and bedded down for the night, the competitors, then dressed in clean shirts and their better

139

jeans, flocked to the Main House for a buffet fit for dignitaries. While musicians played in the atrium, the guests roamed between table after table which were laden with appetizing cuisines.

As soon as the King Ranch shows ended, Little Peppy returned to the cutting pen and also to the winner's circle at both the Crutcher Ranch Cuttings and then the Houston Cutting Horse Association shows, two events held just prior to the NCHA World Championship Finals held in conjunction with the Houston Livestock Show and Rodeo. Little Peppy, like a rifle marksman, had been hitting his own target of winning competitions almost every run. By the time the string of shows were memories, Little Peppy led the NCHA Open show standings with earnings posted in the April *Cuttin' Hoss Chatter* of $19,272.31, almost $7,000 ahead of second place Doc N Willy, a stallion owned by Edwin B. Jones of Redding, California, and shown by Mike Mowery and Tom Lyons. Doc N Willy had won $12,427.54.

"I remember one show at Amarillo before that year was over," reminisced Welch. "Sheila and Shorty were turning back for me. I cut a cow that was just going to run over Little Peppy, but he turned so hard in front of her that it whipped me around. That calf was right up underneath him and when he turned, he hit her hard enough to knock her 10 feet from him. It happened so quick, I didn't realized what he was doing! Then, he just sat down and worked her until the whistle blew. An ordinary horse would have lost that cow, but Little Peppy made a good cow out of her."

ADD THE BREEDING SEASON

With March, however, the schedule changed. Even with a hefty breeding fee of $3,000, an impressive list of mares quickly filled Little Peppy's book. Breeding them took priority over showing.

"For a while there, it was catch-as-catch-can," laughed Toelkes, remembering the hectic schedule of breeding and showing. "Often they would bring Little Peppy by here traveling from one show to another just long enough for us to collect him."

Cuttings more than a half day away from King Ranch, however, were forfeited since collecting the stallion required him to be home every other day for his mares. Welch, with a crew of helpers to obtain what seemed to be the impossible, continued to show the stallion as often as possible. To keep him fit, Little Peppy was exercised daily when back at the Ranch for breeding.

"I can remember one time there was a bunch of cuttings up at Brinkman's," commented Steve Knudsen, discussing the juggling act of breeding and showing Little Peppy at the same time. "As soon as Buster got through with a run, I'd load the horse, and take him back to the Ranch where they'd collect him the next day. Of course, that meant Buster missed that day of showing him. But then I'd load him up after they collected him and return to the show so he could show him the next day. That way Little Peppy didn't miss all of the shows.

"Even after he'd been on a hard trip or back and forth like that, when you saddled him up and stepped him off the next morning, he'd have a hump in his back and he'd be short steppin'," said Knudsen with a grin as he acknowledged liking the stallion's grit. "If you just walked him out, he wouldn't do anything and in about 100 feet, it'd all be gone, but for a minute there it was like a big watermelon under you."

Lank Creacy, like Knudsen, spent his share of time in the driver's seat hauling horses to shows. Early one morning, in preparation for shows held prior to the Houston Livestock Show and Rodeo, he pulled the trailer in front of the barn where Knudsen helped him load it with feed, buckets, hay and tack. They then filled the trailer with an impressive and expensive group of horses.

"I loaded up Little Peppy; Doc O Leo, which was Sheila's horse; Rabbit, the old famous turn-back horse which was a son of El Rey Rojo, along with Tio's show horse and a couple of other show horses," remembered Creacy. "Everybody else was going to be flying in there later. About the time I got

141

ready to leave, Buster slipped up to my truck door and hid a 45 revolver in the door pocket."

Guns played a major role on King Ranch, a means of protection against rattlesnakes and other wild predators when miles away from civilization, but not necessarily on the road. Creacy, with a grin, continued, "Buster had this mischievous look on his face and he asked me, 'You know what that's for? If you wreck and kill one of those horses, that's for you to shoot yourself with.' "

Shortly into the breeding season, it became evident that mixing Little Peppy's two professions of breeding and showing wasn't feasible. According to the May *Cuttin' Hoss Chatter*, Little Peppy had a comfortable lead with $22,692.93, while Doc N Willy had accumulated $16,603.57. The stallion finally remained at the breeding barn to take care of his mares during late spring and early summer while Welch returned to his ranch in Sweetwater to take care of his cattle.

During those months; however, Little Peppy lost his leading edge. In the 122 days from March 15 through July 15, he placed in only 15 shows, and while increasing his earnings to $32,247.52, it wasn't enough to keep distance between himself and second place. Doc N Willy, in a spiraling climb, closed the gap by earning $31,535.50.

In the October *Cuttin' Hoss Chatter*, Peppy San Badger was in second place, having won $34,337.13. Doc N Willy, now $513.64 in the lead, had won $34,850.77. The standings would never reverse. When the year ended, Little Peppy earned the title of Reserve World Champion while Doc N Willy won World Champion. Breeding and showing had not mixed well for Little Peppy.

"The years I hauled Mr San Peppy and bred him, cutting as a sport wasn't as big, so we didn't have as many mares to breed to him," said Welch, comparing his years of hauling the stallions. With Little Peppy, though, he had such a heavy book of mares that we just had to stop showing him and breed mares. There were so many that they bred him into July. After that, when we did start showin' again, I never could bring him back; couldn't get him sharp again. By then, he was out of shape, he seemed to be short-stepping some and it was just so hot. I just couldn't get him back to clickin'."

Little Peppy, however, had clicked well at the breeding barn. During the 1980 breeding season, the stallion bred 119 mares and five of the mares were owned by his own previous owner, Joe Kirk Fulton.

Sheila Welch, riding Peppy San Badger, won their share of championships. Photo by Louise L. Serpa, courtesy of Buster and Sheila Welch.

NCHA HALL OF FAME

In December 1980, 6-year-old Peppy San Badger grabbed one more brass ring when he followed in his sire's footsteps and was inducted into the NCHA Hall of Fame with accumulated earnings of $172,710.52. Interestingly, in 1974, his sire, Mr San Peppy, had achieved that most prestigious accolade when he, too, was a 6-year-old-stallion.

15

PREPARATION FOR BREEDING

"*M*en are generally more careful of the breed of their horses and dogs than of their children.*"*

William Penn

A s the cool breezes of spring turned to the heat of summer, Dr. Toelkes, along with enough hands to keep the flickering flames of fatigue away from his role in starting new foals, performed amazing feats with numbers. Daily he collected, inseminated and tallied more mares than would have been considered feasible only a few years earlier. Part of the reason was credited to modern technology, part to Toelkes' disciplinary attitude toward routine and part to the players of King Ranch.

A FIELD OF DREAMS

As in the early days of Captain King, when the *Kinenos,* skilled as horsemen and cattlemen, used wisdom accumulated from their previous generations to tend to the herds, their great grandsons and great-great grandsons carried on the tradition in the breeding program of Little Peppy.

"I was fortunate that I had Placido and his son, David," began Toelkes, referring to two of the *Kinenos* who helped him as he continually stressed the importance of the hard-working Ranch people in making the breeding program a success. "They were both raised on the Ranch and started working with the vets that were here before World War II. They and men like them helped make this place great. It made no difference if it was weekends or Christmas; if they were supposed to work, they worked."

Toelkes spoke of men like Steve Knudsen and David Trevino, who cared for the stallions; Charlie Shive, who was the broodmare manager until 1982, and then Paul and Jonell Studnicka, who took over their management. There was Frank Posas; Hilario Garza Jr., nicknamed La Le; Hilario Garza III, nicknamed Quincy; Cipriano Garcia, nicknamed Piano; Gabriel Trevino; Danny Miller; Steve Shermer; Emeterio Silguero, Jr.; Rodolfo Q. Silguero, nicknamed Yo Yo; Sylverio Martinez; Robert Reyes; Danny Torres, Jr.; Enrique Falcon, Jr., nicknamed Ricky, and Pat Sprouse (Stiles). These, and others, were a big part of the reason King Ranch emerged as a successful commercial breeding operation.

"Besides good workers, they were horsemen," added Toelkes. "They knew how to handle animals and some of these guys and gals absolutely had a gift for that. They could walk into the stall with the most protective new mother, calm her down, and put a halter on her in no time at all."

THE MARES

As with many breeding operations, climate and shows dictated much of the breeding program at King Ranch. Cold, Arctic winds often slipped as far south as Kingsville, then mingled with the South Texas humidity, seeping deeply into the bones of both man and animal who were accustomed only to heat. The dampness made the cold even more miserable and chilling.

Since some outside mares, as well as King Ranch mares, foaled at the Ranch, Toelkes preferred to not have any January and February foals. He chose to avoid the winter months with its opportunities for illness. Therefore, March marked the beginning of breeding season, after which it was an every-other-day routine, weekends included, until the middle of July. Besides, by March, better weather, the stock shows and several of the larger cutting horse competitions, including the NCHA World Finals, were also over.

As the month approached with hints of spring, horse trailers began lining up behind one another at the Creek Barn, the depositing point for their mares, waiting patiently for an empty trailer to pull away so another could pull up to unload. Here began the systematic approach that guaranteed identification of each mare.

King Ranch broodmares wore white collars while client mares wore yellow collars. Photo courtesy of King Ranch Archives, King Ranch, Inc..

"For me, this time of year was a constant renewal," remembered Janell Kleberg who lived within walking distance of the broodmare facilities, "trailers, raising a cloud of caliche dust, bringing mares to be bred, going to see what mares had arrived and what mares had foaled the night before."

While the new mare viewed her unfamiliar surroundings, Paul Studnicka slipped a numbered, yellow collar around her neck, signifying she was a client mare. Ranch mares wore white collars. Then, with the speed that accompanies years of experience, he swiftly wrapped the collar fasteners with colored duct tape, the color identical to the one assigned to her stallion. Like a newborn baby with an identification bracelet, the mare's collar also had an identification number which was recorded on her record sheet.

"We kept the customer mares separated from the Ranch mares," Studnicka explained. "For the customer mares, unless they preferred them to be in a stall, we grouped about 16 mares in a paddock, depending on their age and the condition of the mares. All of the older mares were put together. You didn't want to put an older mare with the young ones because she'd get pushed away from the feed. We also had paddocks for the seasoned mares and the maiden mares. When we'd get a full paddock, we'd start a new one because we wouldn't mix maiden mares, seasoned mares, and older ones."

One of Toelkes' right-hand men, "La Le" Garza, who helped at the Collection Barn, also assisted Studnicka at the broodmare barn. La Le had been at King Ranch since arriving with his family when he was 17 years old. Even at that young age, he was already a veteran with horses, having worked with his father in Thoroughbred and Quarter Horse stables from California to New York.

One of Toelkes' right-hand men, Hilario (La Le), helping with the breeding. Photo by Janell Kleberg.

"When we got here, I told my brother, 'Oh, boy, now we start working the good horses, but nope, we clean pens,' " grinned La Le. "I liked working for the Ranch, though. It was pretty hard work in those days, but I married and raised my family here."

Garza cared for the horses on King Ranch like they were his children; correcting them as needed, giving them respect mingled with affection, expecting the same in return. "We didn't separate the mares by the stallion they were to be bred to," continued La Le, a *vaquero* whom Toelkes and Studnicka both considered to be gifted in working with horses. "We tried to keep mares, which came in at the same time, together so they could get used to one another. That was more important. If you put a new mare in with a group of established mares, they might fight."

The paddocks, which varied in size from five to nine acres, would also vary in the number of mares it held. While the average was 16, the number depended on new mares coming in and pregnant mares going home. To keep down any problems from a

Mare traps were usually filled with outside mares during the breeding season at King Ranch. Photo courtesy of King Ranch Archives, King Ranch, Inc.

group of mares cohabiting, Garza made sure the big tires, serving as feeders to combat the rust problem of South Texas which metal feeders encounter, remained full of alfalfa around the clock. The horses were also grained daily so that plenty of nourishment kept the mares satisfied, thus removing a primal need to fight for food and providing the necessities that pregnancy requires.

"We did the same thing with the Ranch mares," stated Studnicka. "At one time, we had over 300 Ranch mares running together, but that didn't work too good since some mares would dominate the older ones and the younger ones would keep them back from the hay feeders. Some horses were just more timid than others, so smaller numbers worked better."

While Dr. Toelkes believed herding instincts made mares running together adapt better than those confined, Studnicka and La Le were still assigned close watch on the new mares when they were first put in a paddock. Those which had spent most of their lives at shows and living alone in stalls sometimes had problems learning to socialize. With time, however, all problems usually resolved themselves.

"When mares are allowed to roam together as a herd, they form attachments and bond with one another," explained Toelkes. "They'd get a buddy and keep that buddy with them. It's herd dynamics. They establish their own social order and if we provide them with plenty to eat, they'll do well. If you get much more than 20 mares together; however, it doesn't work as well because they'll often split into smaller groups."

PRELIMINARY BREEDING WORK

Dr Toelkes began his day by 7:00 a.m., stopping first by his office to load his yellow Isuzu truck with everyday requirements of antibiotics, bandages, wound dressings, KY Jelly and sleeves. He also handled the cattle work since the introduction of truck radios, better Ranch roads for traveling quickly from one pasture to another and so many excellent right-hand men, made the job manageable. Before leaving for the Creek Barn, Toelkes took care of necessary office tasks, signed health papers and made notes on yesterday's work and tomorrow's responsibilities. By 8:00 a.m. the yellow Isuzu was parked at the Creek Barn.

"I first went through the barn and took care of any sickness," recalled Toelkes. "We also drew blood on babies foaled during the night to see if they had gotten immunity from their mom's milk. This was the time I did general housekeeping chores, treated the sick, and put on bandages."

While Toelkes attended to general housekeeping, Studnicka concentrated on gathering mares. The daily routine for breeding required mares to pass two tests before reaching the breeding barn. First, they were teased, a process whereby stallions were introduced to the mares to see if the mare would show interest in him. If so, then they were palpated. Those who proved to be cycling were bred that afternoon.

The day's work actually began the evening before for Paul and his wife, Jonell, in order to be ready for the early morning gathering. Paul made two separate sets of teasing charts, paper on which the mares were listed by their numbers for teasing the next day. One chart listed the "wet mares," those mares with foals by their side, while a separate chart listed the "dry" mares, those without foals.

Then, referring to the breeding sheets, statistical records on each mare that were the "bible" in each day's breeding session, Paul also listed mares which were previously bred, and; therefore, should be bred again, adding new mares who had come in heat since the last breeding, those mares which were due a pregnancy check and mares which should be coming in heat. Jonell made a list of the foals that needed to be brought in who were in need of vaccinations that day.

"Jennifer Gold, who worked with us, would bring up two paddocks of wet mares at a time," described Studnicka, "and these mares would be placed in the 24 individual teasing stalls. Silverio Martinez then led a tease stallion along the stalled mares and both Jennifer and I listed the new ones that teased in, the ones to be bred again, those to be pregnancy checked or mares with foals to be vaccinated."

Gold often had help on her early morning gatherings. "I loved to go ride out and help bring the mares and foals to the breeding shed from the paddocks," added Janell Kleberg. "I could hear the cacophony of mares and foals calling each morning across the creek from our home. It was especially beautiful on foggy mornings in the early spring, when the first foals were more interested in chasing each other than going to the barn."

The mares which passed teasing inspection were first turned loose into an alley leading to a holding pen. Even if only two or three mares from a paddock needed breeding, their social order was not disturbed by mixing them with mares from other paddocks. The remainder of the mares who failed to "tease in" were then driven back to their respective paddock. The same process then began with the dry mares.

During the height of breeding season, 22 paddocks a day could be tested, and Toelkes, who began with the client's mares first and ended with King Ranch mares, often palpated as many as 100 mares, still finishing the process by noon. "We were fortunate to have a lot of teasing stallions to use because it got hot and they got tired and mad with so many mares to go through," commented Toelkes. "We had enough teasers; however, to switch them out and keep the program flowing."

A band of King Ranch broodmares during the breeding season. Photo courtesy of King Ranch Archives, King Ranch, Inc.

The King Ranch commercial breeding operation continued to grow yearly, thus requiring the double testing for deciding which mares to breed. While, in 1980, Little Peppy bred 118 mares, in 1981, he bred 146 mares, then 201 mares the following year. During 1985, he bred 299 mares, his largest number during one year. These, however, were Little Peppy mares only and did not include the mares bred to Mr San Peppy or any additional stallion whose mares were artificially inseminated.

"Had there not been so many mares to breed, it wouldn't have been as critical for Doc to palpate everyone that teased," said Paul. "But with that many mares, you had to use the semen that you collected wisely, so he checked them to make sure they were near ovulation before breeding them. A maiden mare and a dry mare, for example, can show heat quite a while before she is ready to be bred."

After the mares were teased and palpated, Paul then updated the breeding sheets on mares to be bred that day. One sheet of long paper had five separate charts made up of 31 columns for the number of days of the month and eight lines for eight months. The chart formed an eight-month calendar in a space of approximately two inches deep by the width of the page. Each chart listed the mare's name, her number, and her owner's name, as well as provided the brand of the horse to which she was to be bred. A 'P,' with a bar underneath it, referred to Little Peppy; a 'lazy P,' one laying down, referred to Mr San Peppy.

Studnicka, using a variety of symbols while keeping a daily running status on each mare. "C" stood for cold, meaning the mare was not cycling and; therefore, was either pregnant or not ready to breed. An "X" identified the days she was bred, while numbers in the blocks then counted down 20 days. If the mare checked pregnant, the square was colored yellow to show a 20-day pregnancy check. A red-colored square meant a full-term pregnancy check. For mares which had a foal by their side, a blue square indicated the date on which the foal had been born.

"That date was essential," stated Paul, "so we'd know when to start teasing the mare to breed her on her foal heat. Mares with a baby by their side can be so protective of their foal that they won't tell you they are in heat when you tease them."

Jonell, a meticulous bookkeeper, later made books from the combination of all the charts, providing a day-by-day diary of the life of each mare. Daily, she logged palpation dates, vaccination records, trimmings, blood tests and medical treatment, as well as a collection of other information. The book, all handwritten, became the hub of the breeding activity and provided information quickly when an owner called.

"Paul and Jonell ran it like a big nursery," described Janell Kleberg of the broodmare facilities. "They knew every mare and foal by name and most had nicknames according to their personalities. They even sat up at night to nurse them. There was one orphan born to a mare too old to raise a foal that followed Brian Studnicka, their son, around like a puppy."

WALL CHART

It happened every time. As if pulled by a magnet, an owner's eyes automatically darted to the wall left of the door when entering Studnicka's office. A large chart updated daily, colorfully displayed the checks and balances of teasing charts and breeding sheets; it changed each month, a new poster taking the priority spot and the previous month moving beneath it. The charts made reading about the mares easy.

"This way, you knew exactly what every mare was doing," explained Jonell Studnicka. "Red meant pregnant; black meant the mare was open and yellow meant a 20-day pregnancy check. People liked to look at their mare's record." Then, with eyes twinkling, she added, "But they also wanted to see who else was breeding to the same stallion as them.

Just like the breeding, the record keeping demanded hours of work. To keep the program running as problem free as possible, Jonell and Paul arrived at the Creek Barn every morning by 6:30 a.m., often not leaving before 11:00 that night. "Others could have helped and posted the books and chart," admitted Jonell, "but if you don't do it yourself, you don't retain what's going on with that horse."

Usually by noon, morning preparation was over. With the mares either in the holding pens to be bred or already returned to their paddocks, lunch, whatever the hour, provided a break, separating prep time from afternoon breeding. Rather than eat; however, it was a time for Dr. Toelkes to get ready for the afternoon session. After swinging by the office to take care of any pressing business, Toelkes went to the Collection Barn. Every breeding afternoon meant a busy afternoon.

16

THE BUSINESS OF CREATION

1975: opened commercial breeding program
1978: First year to breed Little Peppy
1985: largest booking to outside mares with 342 outside mares
  bred to all three stallions: Little Peppy, Mr San Peppy and Dry Doc.
1985: 299 mares bred to Little Peppy, the largest number in one year
1992: last year for Ranch breeding

It was imperative; a breeding day had to click like a grandfather clock, no hesitations, no stopping. The morning was designated as a time to separate the stock into workable groups; the afternoon for breeding. To accomplish the tasks required eight full-time employees with approximately 14 additional employees who worked during peak breeding season.

BRINGING THE STALLIONS

While Toelkes prepared for the afternoon session at the octagonal-shaped Collection Barn, Steve Knudsen, as soon as he finished eating, retrieved the first stallion for collecting. For several years, King Ranch stood a variety of third stallions; at one time Doc Holiday, then later Dry Doc and finally CJ Sugar. The third stallion lived at the same end of the barn with Mr San Peppy while Little Peppy lived at the other. Knudsen had developed a routine which worked well with all of his stallions, a routine he credited to his days of working with Stanley Glover when mares were live covered.

"These were easy stallions to handle," acknowledged Knudsen. "We had girls that worked here loping colts, and they could do anything they wanted to with Mr San Peppy and Little Peppy; they were just that well-mannered. We usually had a barn full of mares in training stalled in the barn with them, but that didn't make any difference. They didn't squeal or make noises in the barn, so, when I took them on the first part of the walk to the Collection Barn, I expected them to be well-mannered, also.

"Of course," he continued, "they knew where they were going, so when we turned the corner by some houses, about

Steve Knudsen in the breeding barn. Photo courtesy of King Ranch Archives, King Ranch, Inc.

halfway to the Collection Barn, I'd let them act like studs. Even after that, though, I didn't let them act up too much or get too carried away."

Smiling at the memory, he continued, "Little Peppy acted more the stallion than any of them. There was a place, always by the loading chute on the way to the Collection Barn, where I'd have to get on to him that first year. He was a smart horse, though, and after that year, it all became routine. He'd act mannerly until we rounded those houses, and then prance and snort and carry on, but after a few years, anyone could have handled him."

Preparing for the day's breeding at King Ranch. Photo courtesy of King Ranch Archives, King Ranch, Inc.

While Knudsen brought the first stallion, Toelkes warmed the collection thermoses, wide-mouth bottles in which a plastic whirl pac could be placed and then sealed. These receptacles housed the semen for transportation to the breeding barn. To guarantee no mistakes, each colored thermos, a different color for each stallion, also had color-coded tape on its lid to match its thermos. Both thermos and lid then matched the tape on the mare's collar who would receive the semen.

"There was a microscope at the collection barn and every day Doc looked at the semen and appraised it," continued Knudsen. "We had machines that read the sperm count, so when we knew how many mares we had to breed, Doc then knew how much extender to add to the semen. This was repeated with every collection."

After the first two stallions were collected, Dr. Toelkes sent the colored thermos bottles to Paul Studnicka at the breeding barn, who started the breeding process rolling. "We usually always had three stallions to collect," said Toelkes. "I tried to use the same sequence every time by collecting any other stallion, like Doc Holiday or Dry Doc, first; Mr San Peppy next, and then Little Peppy last. Little Peppy always had the most mares to breed. By the time I finished collecting him, I took his thermos to the breeding barn and helped breed his mares. They usually had the mares that were being bred by the other stallions finished by that time."

Toelkes believed heavily in routine, striving to keep the same schedule at the same time each day. "I believe that a horse does better when kept in a daily routine than when that routine is disturbed. If you feed them the same time every day, they expect that and feel comfortable with it. In fact, those in the pasture will act just like dairy cattle and come to the fence about the time they are suppose to get fed. It was the same thing with breeding. When we could stay with a routine, the same, day in and day out, everything worked easier."

APPLYING NATURE

While the breeding people worked hard to keep a constant routine, the climate, however, did not always cooperate. Since it could be a substantial change from home, Toelkes expected the mares to need time to adjust to the climate.

"This is a very harsh climate in many ways and while a horse is adaptable to cold, they're less adaptable to heat," explained Toelkes. "The long days of sun, however, have their advantages. We bred horses that

157

came from all over the United States without using lights to help them cycle because we had plenty of sunshine to do that. We had a lot of big-named mares that we boarded year-round as well, so they didn't have to adjust to the climate. Besides helping the mare owner with transportation costs, it also helped us keep our people year round working horses."

Mother Nature could be just as harsh on the young foals at their birth as she had been on the mares at their arrival. Unaware of the dangers of the austere sun on newborn foals, Toelkes experienced the problem first-hand in the early years at King Ranch.

"We found that when a mare had a new foal," Toelkes continued, "we had to keep her and the baby in a stall for a couple of days, particularly late spring-born foals, because the foals lacked resistance to heat. We had a mare who was in a lot by herself to foal one night. Everything was fine the next morning, but that day the mare stayed out in the sun and her new baby laid out in the sun with her. Now we were around her all day long and thought nothing of this. You see older foals lay out while their mothers graze all the time, so we assumed the baby was sleeping. That evening, though, we found it dead due to excessive heat.

"Since then," he continued, "I have found the same thing to be true with baby calves. Cows and mares don't have the instinct to protect newborn babies from the sun. Female deer, however,

John Toelkes with Little Peppy at the breeding barn. Photo by Janell Kleberg put their baby in the shade."

PREPARING LITTLE PEPPY

Little Peppy first began breeding as a 4-year-old and took to the art of breeding a "dummy," an artificial mare, without any problem. Before

Inside the breeding barn at King Ranch. Photo courtesy King Ranch Archives, King Ranch, Inc.

mounting the dummy, however, he expected the teaser mares to offer him the right enticement. Although still on a long shank, Little Peppy had his freedom in the Collection Barn where three mares stood in stocks for him to visit. While Knudsen took him to the first mare and then backed away, rarely did Little Peppy accept this mare, at least not at first. Instead, he pranced up and down in front of the three mares, preferring to be choosy about the one he wanted to court, definitely showing preferences for some mares over others.

"He had a little quirk," smiled Knudsen. "If the teasing mares were going out of their cycle rather than hot, it took longer to collect him. You might even have to get a fresh set of mares in the stalls in order to get him

159

collected. If she had just come in heat, he'd be ready to collect faster. Maybe it was instinct; maybe he knew if they were in the pasture she would accept him and the others wouldn't. He was funny like that"

Toward the end of breeding season, when most mares were bred and only stragglers remained, finding a mare just starting her heat cycle to entice Little Peppy could pose a problem. Toelkes preferred to not use mares with colts to encourage the stallions, not wanting to take the chance of getting a baby hurt. Sometimes, however, they were the only available 'hot' mares, since having foaled late, they would be in foal heat. Then, in order to get Little Peppy collected, a wet mare belonging to the Ranch was brought in.

COMPARING FATHER AND SON

Just as Little Peppy was more the artisan in the show pen, Mr San Peppy was more the work horse in the breeding barn. "Mr San Peppy wasn't particular about his mares like Little Peppy," compared Knudsen. "You could even use a set of mares that wouldn't work for Little Peppy and collect Mr San Peppy without any problem."

Toelkes agreed. "Mr San Peppy was all business, a very skilled workman. There wasn't any pizzazz or flash, with him; it was, 'Let's get the job done;' five minutes and he was out of there."

Raising his eyebrows, he added, "But you knew better than to expect that from Little Peppy. Little Peppy was more artistic, he liked to fool around a little bit more. They looked that way, they acted that way in the show pen and they were that way in the breeding barn. Neither one of them ever missed a collection, though, in the 13 years I bred them and only a few times did they have to mount the dummy more than once. They were well-trained breeding horses."

BACK TO THE BARN: STALLION CARE

Even after the end of his show career, Little Peppy continued to live in a spacious 12 x 12 stall of cool mortar and wire in the wide-alleyed barn. Joe Stiles made the decision to house him there rather than in a paddock, since he had spent the majority of his life in a stall. His regimen, however, included more than just looking out from its door.

An aerial shot of Creek Barn and King Ranch's breeding facilities. Photo courtesy of King Ranch Archives, King Ranch, Inc.

Activity of one kind or another kept him occupied for most of the day. Every morning, David Trevino took him from his stall and thoroughly brushed him; later, he was exercised and, after returning from the Collection Barn, given a bath. When it wasn't breeding season, bathing was usually an every-other-day occurrence.

Knudsen, who shod Little Peppy, also oversaw his nutritional needs as

161

well, keeping a close eye on the feeding routine to ensure that feeding changed with the needs of the horse. A sign on the wall showed the scoop measurements, while gray masking tape beside the latch on his stall gave instructions about which scoop measurement to use. The same system was used on all horses in the barn, with the gray duct tape making change easy.

"We fed the horses according to what they needed, not according to a set amount," he explained. "We didn't feed them three scoops of grain every day just because that's what they had been eating. I tried to feed at least once a day myself and changed the feed instructions as needed to keep up their condition, but not let them get too fat."

Horse care, especially during breeding season, was a meticulous daily routine that had to be tended to, no matter how you felt or where you wanted to be; yet, those who were a part of the King Ranch breeding team didn't mind. In fact, they seemed to become a part of it, preferring the fast-paced world of procreation, amid torrid heat and bone-tiring long hours, to days in an air-conditioned office overlooking a world of concrete.

Toelkes best summed up the sentiments of King Ranch employees: "You get caught up in it; it gets in your blood, and there's no other way."

17

COLIC

G ail Newman knew Little Peppy. She knew he loved affection and was usually fed two flakes of alfalfa and two scoops of sweet feed twice a day; she knew he'd nicker at her at feeding time or perhaps when wanting a little attention, and she also knew he knew when to stand very still and quiet when he needed help.

"I was sweeping out the barn at end of a day," recalled Gail. "We swept away from the stalls to the center of the alleyway and then vacuumed down the middle. The stalls had two doors, one to the alleyway and another to an outside gate at the back of it. I noticed Little Peppy was by the outside gate toward the back, standing very quietly. It was really kind of unusual, since he liked people and stayed at the front gate a lot when we were in there working, but I didn't think much about it.

Paying little attention to the stallion, Gail continued her sweeping, finishing one side, then crossing over to sweep the other. Suddenly, the swishing movements of her broom, frequently hitting the meshwire stall doors, startled both her and an enemy lying concealed inside Little Peppy's stall.

"A rattlesnake was coiled up right there on the inside of the mesh door," said Gail. "And, of course, I jumped away, and ran for help immediately. Little Peppy, though, stayed in his corner of the stall, away from that snake and remained real quiet until somebody came to rescue him."

It happened about 1:30 p.m., July 19, 1985. July always encased South Texas in a steamy, blistering heat, seldom broken by rains, only periodically abated by southerly breezes, and those usually so scorching, they offered little relief. July wasn't anyone's favorite month. It was the month that symbolized the middle of the long, hot summers, often as not, accompanied by droughts.

October was a favorite month with its hint of fall. So was November with its teasing rains, as were March or April when the birds once again chirped and an enjoyable briskness lay in the air, refusing to allow the mind to remember Julys. Until around 1:30 p.m. that afternoon, nothing had been different about that day. Breeding for the day had ended, La Le Garza was returning the last mares to their paddocks, Jonell Studnicka was busily updating her charts and Dr. Toelkes was checking mares to see if they were pregnant. Then, it happened.

SURGERY #1

As one who worked daily from early morning to late afternoon in the Thoroughbred Barn, Gail Newman had become accustomed to the habits of each of the horses standing there. Like living with one's children, she had unconsciously developed an eye for peculiarities that signaled a soreness or a pain.

As she went about her chores on the afternoon of July 19, she casually glanced toward Little Peppy and immediately sensed something was wrong. A short time earlier, he had been bathed after returning from the collection barn and seemed fine then, but now, as she walked quickly to his stall, Gail sensed, rather than saw, something was wrong.

Quickly, she flipped the latch on the Little Peppy's stall door, stepped inside, and realized Little Peppy was trying to lie down. Wetness glistened on his neck and partially covered his back. She knew the wetness was definitely not from his bath; by now, Little Peppy should be dry. This wetness was the sweat of pain and this was the sign of colic.

"I ran and got Mike," remembered Gail. "He was a college graduate who worked there for a short time and was like the barn manager. We got Little Peppy out of the stall and I started walking him while Mike ran to get Dr. Toelkes. I knew he didn't feel good; at times it seemed like colic, but at times it didn't."

"Little Peppy was in his stall on the southwest corner of the barn when I got up there," remembered Toelkes. "It was evident he was in a lot of pain so I immediately treated him to relieve the pain, expecting it to give him relief in a short time. Then I gave him some laxatives to help induce a bowel movement, but nothing I did seemed to ease him so I decided we'd take him for a ride. I'd found over the years in my vet practice that clients would say they were bringing in a horse which was severely colicking, but by the time they brought him over those rough Ranch roads, and backwoods, farm-to-market roads, they'd have a bowel movement and be okay."

Toelkes, hoping the swaying motion of riding in the trailer would do the same now for Little Peppy, loaded him in an in-line trailer; then he, along with Stiles and Knudsen, trailered the stallion along a road that looped around the Ranch. The trip, however, brought no relief. After unloading him back at headquarters, even with the amount of pain killer administered to Little Peppy, stress still flickered in his eyes, while attempts to lie down and periodic quivering removed any doubt that the stallion's pain had not subsided.

"We took him behind the headquarters to this big, grassy area to walk him," remembered Knudsen, "but it didn't help him any. In fact, he seemed to be getting worse. He'd walk a few steps and then grab himself and act like he wanted to go down again."

"Mike and I did the walking," recalled Gail. "We'd alternate; I'd lead him for a while and Mike would be behind keeping him going, then we'd change places. You could look at him and tell he was sick, but he would walk fine for a couple of steps. Then all of a sudden, he'd have a spasm and almost fall down."

As the minutes ticked away without any signs of relief, the knot Toelkes had first felt in the pit of his stomach when loading the stallion for his ride, grew larger and larger. He knew Little Peppy had a serious problem and it was time to go for help. Like a drill sergeant, Toelkes spouted instructions to those with him, then hurried to the office, his mind clicking off people to call before getting on the road with the stallion. Every minute was critical now; none could be wasted. He glanced at his watch. Almost 3:00 p.m.

"Doc really made a quick call." said Knudsen, "That's what helped the horse survive. He didn't get any infection in there. We were also lucky it happened in the daytime; had Little Peppy gotten sick in the evening, when nobody was here to find him, it would have been bad."

While Mike and Gail forced Little Peppy to walk, Stiles and Knudsen hooked a trailer to Perry Finger's dually, the truck parked closest that was capable of hauling a trailer to College Station quickly. They then loaded the stallion and some emergency vet supplies.

"By then, there were plenty of people here to help load him," remembered Gail. "Usually he liked to get in the trailer and go, but when they tried to load him then, he hurt so bad that he wasn't easy to load him."

Toelkes, in the meantime, called Texas A & M University, the home of a teaching veterinary college, at least six hours from Kingsville on a normal drive. Anxiously tapping the desk as he waited for the call to go through, he made a mental note of another phone call that Joe Stiles needed to make. It would make the trip faster.

"We had good help in getting Little Peppy to A & M," he acknowledged. "Joe called our Kleberg County Sheriff, Jim Scarborough, who called ahead and the law enforcement left us alone; they even escorted us through Halletsville." Then, with a rueful smile he added, "On the north side of Halletsville; however, there was a DPS trooper who hadn't been advised.

166

He stopped us and gave us a ticket."

The men made several other quick stops along the way, each time to administer more pain medication to Little Peppy in an effort to keep the stallion as easy as possible. Almost before Stiles rolled to a stop on the side of the road, Toelkes, a syringe full of pain killer in hand, leaped from the truck, took three long strides and then agilely jumped on the trailer's running board. Jerking open the trailer's side door, he swiftly administered more pain reliever to the stallion, then just as quickly jumped back in the truck already in a slow roll as Stiles pulled away from the shoulder of the road. Time could not be wasted.

Shortly before 8:00 p.m., as the sun slowly sank in the western sky, Stiles pulled the trailer up to the large animal clinic at Texas A & M where two surgeons, Dr. Tex Taylor and Dr. Jeff Watkins, accompanied by Dr. Leon Scrutchfield, were waiting. By 10:00 p.m., Little Peppy was undergoing surgery.

Dr. John Toelkes, the veterinarian at King Ranch. Photo by Janell Kleberg.

"Joe and I paced the floor while we waited for the surgery room to be prepared," stated Toelkes. "That's all we could do and it was plenty nerve racking. When surgery finally got under way, we watched it and as someone periodically gave us a report, Joe would then call Tio who stayed by the phone at the Ranch."

It didn't take long for the surgeons to find the problem, a piece of discolored intestine, but since it was not badly discolored, they deferred the call to remove it to Toelkes.

"There was a 50/50 chance that they could leave the intestine and it would be alright. If the intestine didn't function though, they'd have to go

167

back in, so I said 'take the gut'; that's what they wanted to hear. I felt if the intestine had been deprived of oxygen or fresh blood long enough to discolor it, then this piece might not be fully functional, so he might colic again; or he might have to live on a special diet and we didn't want that. Little Peppy, until that moment, had been a young, healthy horse."

Shortly before midnight, and an hour and a half after beginning the surgery, Dr. Tex Taylor and Dr. Jeff Watkins, tired but pleased with the surgery, planned the post operative care. Little Peppy was now resting well. Relieved, Stiles made one more call to Tio. Then as tiredness overtook their previous adrenaline-fed anxiety, he and Toelkes went in search of a motel room, ready for rest themselves.

"It was a week, that seemed like an eternity, before it was determined that Little Peppy would survive," remembered Janell Kleberg. "It wasn't just the thought of losing a great stallion, it was the sympathy that we all felt for him." Thoughtfully she added, "Little Peppy loved to be cared for by sweet young girls; he thrived on their affection, and I guess it probably saved his life."

The next day, after seeing Little Peppy, and knowing his condition was now out of their hands, Toelkes and Stiles returned to Kingsville. Brad Abel, an employee of King Ranch, took their place at Texas A & M University, becoming Little Peppy's personal caretaker while he convalesced at the clinic. Abel's only job was to walk, graze and generally care for the stallion which had helped catapult King Ranch into present-day equine history. By late August, Little Peppy, appearing none the worse for his episode, was once again loping the Thoroughbred track.

SURGERY #2

For the next seven years, the stallion remained healthy. In the minds of the people who experienced the harrowing day; the memories of July 19 slowly faded from one filled with minute, vivid details, to settling under overlaying layers of dust. On November 19, 1992; however, it took only one jolting burst of action to scattered the dust from their memories, exposing the raw nerves of July 19, 1985, as the day, almost verbatim, repeated itself.

November had chased away the searing summer heat, bringing in its place some cool refreshing days of autumn. Like the weather, plans were also changing at King Ranch. Next year, instead of a commercial breeding operation, King Ranch was closing its doors to outside mares and even sending its stallions to two separate breeding farms.

"We were reducing the number of our broodmares," explained Toelkes. "While the breeding fees from Little Peppy were supporting the entire Quarter Horse program, we could foresee that these monies were going to diminish in the future. We decided that we could realize more money from the breeding operation by sending the stallions to other commercial breeding farms, so the cost of the overhead would be divided among more stallions. With just Little Peppy's income paying the bills, the overhead was rather steep. In addition, we felt moving Little Peppy to Weatherford would put him closer to the 'mare power.' "

This time, Ranch employee, Oscar Longoria, found Little Peppy ill. Longoria went by the barn in the early afternoon to say goodbye to the stallions. Since Mr San Peppy had already left, he approached Little Peppy's stall and found the stallion down, looking back at his flank and trying to roll. Immediately recognizing the horse was not well, he ran to headquarters to summon help.

As Toelkes hurried to the barn, he admitted to himself that the news that Little Peppy was sick surprised him in one respect, but not in another. For awhile, he had noticed that the stallion had not been himself, but he attributed it to him being 18 years old and the slowing down of his reproductive organs.

"We were experiencing a loss of reproductive efficiency with him," recalled John. "He was not as fertile in 1992 as he had been in 1991. Both his total sperm numbers and his live sperm count was dropping markedly."

The men coaxed the stallion up, then Toelkes performed the same treatment as seven years before. Like then, Little Peppy received no relief. Once again he loaded the stallion in a trailer and drove him around the Ranch, trying to relax him enough to have a bowel movement, but again, no results. With Little Peppy's past history, Toelkes did not hesitate for long.

"Doc came to the office and said Little Peppy was sick," stated Kleberg. "He was headed to A & M with him again. It scared all of us. That he had survived one surgery was fortunate; to survive two would be close to a miracle."

Toelkes felt like he was reliving a dream, or rather a nightmare. Once again, as Stiles loaded the stallion, he called Texas A & M University Veterinary College of Medicine. The same team of doctors who operated on Little Peppy seven years earlier, plus an additional doctor, Dr. Rouff, would be waiting.

"It was a miserable trip, a lot of mental stress between here and there," said Toelkes. "The roads were congested, the weather was misty; a lot had changed in seven years that just made the trip between Kingsville and A & M more difficult."

Then to top it off, the stallion, even with the pain killer, received little relief and finally managed to get down in the trailer. "I don't know if it was that he was so tired or in that much pain, but when we stopped to administer pain medicine in Schulenburg, he was down in the trailer." continued Toelkes. "We just left him there since he was confined and couldn't roll. The main reason for keeping them up and walking is to keep them from rolling and causing more problems."

For Kleberg, waiting by the telephone was an emotional roller coaster. One minute agitation overwhelmed him because the phone sat silent, with no news; the next minute, he feared the thought of it ringing, knowing well that the news could be bad. Sleep that night was out of the question.

"I remember waiting for the phone call. Tio sat, without talking, in his

170

favorite chair," described Janell. "His father's worn hat hangs on a hook on the wall not too far from the chair; it reminds us not to expect this business to be easy. The atmosphere at the house was very somber. Little Peppy's illness, though, affected more than just our household. The fabric of this agricultural community is woven very tightly. We all share the joys and the sorrows, so there was an eerie silence here for several days, waiting to see if Little Peppy was going to live."

When the call finally came that night, it was not a good one. "John finally called in the early hours of the morning and said they had to perform surgery; there was no alternative. He also cautioned that Little Peppy might die during the surgery, but he'd surely die without it.

"It's not the surgery that causes death," said Tio, "but the fact that by the time you relieve the symptoms, there's so much internal damage that the horse can't overcome it. Little Peppy, though, miraculously pulled through again."

While Little Peppy survived the surgery, being seven years older than he was when he had his first one, made him more of a surgical risk in 1992 than he had been in 1985. In addition, Toelkes had recently pulled an extensive amount of weight from him in an experimental program.

"We were trying some different things to see if we could rejuvenate his reproductive capacity and in doing so, we'd taken a lot of weight off him, so he was thin. Because of that, his age, and because they had to enter his abdomen through the old surgical scar, he didn't bounce back as fast from surgery the second time."

Although a survivor, the illness, as well as the attempted rejuvenation program, took its toll on Little Peppy's physical condition. His once shiny coat lost its luster; the muscular physique of only a year earlier disappeared to reveal ribs rippling like waves on each side of his body and hip bones protruding like lone mountains. Little Peppy looked the part of an abused horse.

"We immediately put him on a special diet," explained Toelkes of their battle to improve Little Peppy. "We fed him all kinds of things to try to put weight on him. We gave him half a dozen eggs with his feed, and he'd have egg yolk everywhere; he really liked those eggs. Only a few months earlier, he had been fat as a town dog, and now he looked like a mangy puppy. But, with time, we were able to build him up so that he looked somewhat respectable when he was moved to Bullard's.

"Surviving two of these surgeries says a lot for his character and stamina," he continued. "The horse did not fight any of it; he was very accepting of all of this. He just gritted his teeth and stood it."

THEORY

Toelkes, embracing his "routine theory," wondered if changes at the Ranch prior to Little Peppy's colic episodes could have influenced the illness. "A horse does better with a regular routine than almost any other animal. If the sun comes up over that tree while the food is getting tossed into the bucket, he's content. Change the routine and you do damage. It just so happened that the week after Dry Doc arrived and was put on the other end of the barn, Little Peppy got sick and had to have his first abdominal surgery."

Toelkes once again offered a theory on what might have influenced the second illness of Little Peppy. "About this time we had begun letting tourists come through the barn every day and although they couldn't touch him, there was a continuous stream of people flowing by. I think the horse wasn't getting enough rest and that affected him.

"We had also just made the arrangements for Mr San Peppy to go stand at the Lazy E in Guthrie, Oklahoma, and for Little Peppy to go stand at Bullard's in Weatherford. A few days after that, the horse required a second abdominal surgery. There's lots about the social order among horses that we don't understand and I firmly believe we unknowingly cause many of their problems."

BASKING IN GLORY

18

THE GLORIOUS SALE DAYS

"E verybody looks and acts like he's come on out to the Ranch for a show and a barbecue lunch - which is literally true for most of us. There are honchos and multi-millionaires and up-from-hardpan padrones among us, for sure - those Learjets don't belong to the Coast Guard - and presumably their hawk-eyes are intent upon some prize piece of undervalued animal flesh, but you can't spot them just by peering around. Well, not often. John Connally is always going to be a dead ringer for John Connally, and there are two fellers over there wearing Resistols, dark glasses and navy blue suits, and somebody else is awfully well-barbered and just a little smug in the gait. Then, too, it's hard to miss the women. There probably has never been a big rancher so unassuming and down home and unswervingly hard-scrabble that his wife didn't still find a good hairdresser and somebody to tailor her blouses."

"Blood and Money at the King Ranch Auction"
by Richard Boeth in Westward, a special section of the
Nov. 16, 1980 Dallas Times Herald.

174

Each year, as the cooler months nipped at the dog days of summer, King Ranch began preparation for its annual King Ranch Equine and Cattle Sale. The growing fame of Mr San Peppy and Little Peppy added even more luster to the affair, the sale of their progeny igniting contagious expectations of future cutting horse champions. Many came to buy the best colt King Ranch had to offer, hoping it would be the next Peppy San Badger. Some came, not to take home the dream of a champion, but to take home a piece of the rock, a piece of history to later share with their grandchildren. Others came to experience the rich heritage of a distinguished Ranch that, otherwise, they would never encounter.

GETTING READY

"The excitement of getting them all together to grade and screen horses for the sale was like Christmas!" smiled Janell Kleberg. "The breeding barn was close quarters and we all crowded around a long wooden table with these large leather bound books of registration papers. The mares were brought in one at a time, foals scampered behind and had to be coaxed out for us to get a look at them. There were so many great mares, champions, renowned cow horses, all shuffling gently with their foals through that small space in the barn."

The ledger books provided them with a wealth of information. On one side was listed the foals a mare produced every year, how each foal was graded at seven months of age, and if there had been any sales: the purchaser and the price. On the other side of that page was the pedigree. Besides Tio and Joe Stiles, Dr. Toelkes and Paul Studnicka also joined the screening to share any problems that might have occurred during breeding or foaling. Kleberg and Stiles then graded the foals: top, good, fair, fairly-good ("It was like a C plus," explained Tio) or poor; afterwards they assigned the mares to stallions for breeding. It was only the beginning of

175

determining the best offspring for the annual King Ranch Auction.

Months before the sale, the process began again. Kleberg and Stiles spent hours reviewing paper work and viewing fillies and colts. Besides good marks on paper, the hunt was on for a sparkle in an eye, a darting movement or a presence that set some colts apart from others. When the group was finally selected, the best King Ranch had to offer was put in the sale.

"If there were two colts that had equal bloodlines," explained Knudsen, "we sold the one with exceptionally outstanding eye appeal, the one with the chrome, the one that looked the best, and we kept the other."

King Ranch's philosophy for excellence began over 100 years earlier and required broad shoulders from each generation to carry the goals forward. Premium marketing of the best stock was a primary way of caring on the tradition, heralding the Ranch as not only a productive business but also one of honor.

The theory worked. With time, the reputation of progeny grew and the Ranch erected a steel-covered arena across from its *Santa Gertrudis* Headquarters. There, once a year, the

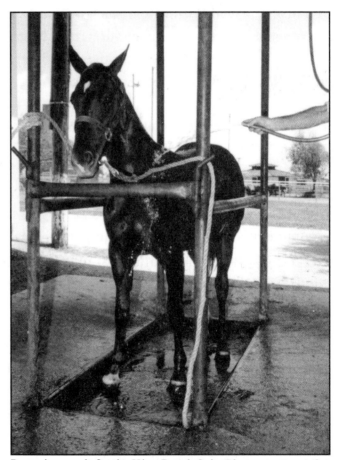

Preparing a colt for the King Ranch Sale. Photo courtesy of King Ranch Archives, King Ranch, Inc.

"best of the best" brought some of the heftiest prices in the industry. The sale ring, its dirt thick and fluffy for prancing young yearlings, sat in the east end of the arena, a rope distinguishing it from the remainder of the area. Chairs and bleachers covered the rest of the arena where its dirt was packed as hard as concrete.

Even with a bumper crop of chairs so closely aligned, they seemed attached, people still overflowed into bleachers lining the sides of the covered arena, squeezing together tightly. Those with no place to sit hunted room between the bleachers, behind them, to the side of them or where ever enough space allowed a pair of boots to stand.

Weeks prior to the event, King Ranch employees feverishly tackled their annual job of refurbishing and painting, mowing and trimming as well as cleaning and putting up. In addition, they bathed and brushed horses; then they did it again, fitting them for their first performance to a scrutinizing public. Loyalty ran deep at King Ranch. With so many people coming to its annual sales, it was imperative that the horses look good, the Ranch look immaculate and the hospitality be the best. King Ranch employees saw to that.

"We'd start before daylight," remembered Knudsen, "and we did a lot of walking to get everyone of those horses tended to! We took the sale colts, which were in two different barns, to the treadmill where they were exercised for 15 minutes; after that we washed them and brushed them. If things went right, we'd have all the sale colts done by noon."

THE DAY BEFORE

Rather than making it a one-day affair, spectators and buyers alike flocked into Kingsville several days prior to the noted event. King Ranch put on cutting demonstrations the day before the Sale, first exhibiting offspring from Ranch stallions who had excelled in the cutting ring, then displaying the 3-year-old prospects that they would be showing in the NCHA Futurity. Trained and almost ready for the show only six weeks away, the young, hopeful winners displayed their talent under the scrutinizing eye of the public. Finally, for the grand finale, Mr San Peppy and Little Peppy both performed.

SALE DAY

The next day, even more trucks with trailers and Cadillacs with Stetson-hatted drivers passed one another on Highway 77, headed to King Ranch while up above, the gentle hum of aircraft signaled other means of arrival. The skies at times

Tio Kleberg and Jack Anderson, both past presidents of AQHA, preparing for sale talks. Photo courtesy of King Ranch Archives, King Ranch, Inc.

resembled gridlock as Lear jets and Cessnas circled, impersonating eagles tipping and turning, patiently spiraling above their target and waiting their opportunity to sweep down onto an unseen airstrip. Although it was still hours before the gavel would make a resounding thud, announcing the sale of the first yearling, prospective buyers were eager to roam the Ranch and examine the wares.

"In front of the sale barn," remembered horseman Louis Pearce of Rosharon, Texas, a frequent prospective buyer at King Ranch sales, "they had each one of the sale horses outside with a handler. There

Norias Ranch cook, Apolinar Amador (Borado), cooking rice at a Ranch Sale. Photo courtesy of King Ranch Archives, King Ranch, Inc.

178

would be about 25 horses and handlers spread up and down the area, making it easy for you to walk around the colts and really get a good look at them. It was a good way to view them."

Just as the sale colts were out on display, Mr San Peppy and Little Peppy, coats shining and muzzles shaved, stood outside on the luscious, green grass like regal Kings subliminally suggesting the offspring nearby would one day be as grand. Knudsen and Garza usually manned the stallions and although they were kept relatively close to one another, they acted like gentlemen.

THE LATE 70'S KING RANCH AUCTIONS

"I remember a mare named Peppy's Tigre who was the first Mr San Peppy filly to sell in the Ranch Sale," said Knudsen, reflecting on a red-dun filly out of Tiger Bars 2. "Earlier that year, we were hauling a couple of halter horses around to the AQHA shows and we took her along with a filly by Double L Straw. They were two totally different-looking horses. The look of the Double L Straw filly was what was getting marked those days, so we thought we had a chance of winning with her; we just hoped to place the Mr San Peppy filly somewhere."

With a big wide grin, he added, "I'll never forget that show. Peppy Tigre surprised 'em all by winning the class; I beat some of the big-name trainers with that filly."

Just as she stirred up the AQHA halter class, Peppy Tigre stirred up the buyers at the 1976 King Ranch auctions when she sold for $26,000. She was the highest-selling yearling in the Sale and was purchased by Country Store Gallery Inc.

The next year, 1977, from the 29 lots offered in the 26th annual auction, seven progeny sired by Mr San Peppy sold, averaging $14,714. Mr San Peppy had remained a topic of conversation all year and by the end of that year, he set the record as the all-time open cutting money winner. Peppy Brooks, the high-selling horse, bringing $20,000, was purchased by Tom and Suzanne Warner of Las Vegas, Nevada.

The high-selling colt of the 1979 King Ranch Sale was Peppys T Shirt, a yearling stallion, bringing $17,000 from Earl Abels of Ralls, Texas. Photo by Janell Kleberg.

By 1978, Little Peppy set the stage for that year's auction of Mr San Peppy progeny, having won the 1977 NCHA Futurity as well as the 1978 NCHA Derby. Fifteen Mr San Peppy offspring went through the ring.

The following year, 1979, 19 yearlings sold. It was a good year financially. Gold reached a record $524 per ounce, up from $223 in 1978. With growing purses in the cutting arena and the growing recognition of bloodlines, the success of Mr San Peppy's progeny from the year before emerged as free advertisement in selling horses; the technique worked especially well for the prominent King Ranch, both by private treaty and at the auctions.

While Little Peppy primed the 1979 sale by winning the 1978 NCHA

Derby, SOLTERA PEPPY, another Mr San Peppy offspring, followed on his heels, splitting 4th through 7th places in the 1978 NCHA Futurity. There were two offspring, sired by a two-time World Champion, one winning a major event and the other making the finals in a major event, making Mr San Peppy's foals look as much like a "sure bet" for the cutting arena as betting on the sun coming up in the morning.

Janell Kleberg and her 10-year-old son, Jay, at a King Ranch Sale. Photo courtesy of King Ranch Archives, King Ranch, Inc..

Peppys T Shirt, purchased by Earl Abels of Ralls, Texas, bringing $17,000, proved the public's faith in his progeny. The 19 yearlings that sold, all sired by Mr San Peppy, averaged $11,111.11. In the wings was Little Peppys first crop of colts.

19

SALES IN THE 80'S AND 90'S

W ith the financial records of the world on public display for 1979, **Fortune Magazine** noted that Exxon emerged as the largest Corporation for the year with sales of $79,106,471,000. In 1933, Bob Kleberg secured a lease with Humble Oil Company, whose name later changed to Exxon Oil Company. They still hold the lease to the oil flowing beneath King Ranch soil; it does not expire until the year 2013.

In 1980, American politics wrapped itself up in the election of Ronald Reagan as the United States President. At the same time, King Ranch was involved in the restructuring of its own Ranch hierarchy. The last Ranch patriarch, Dick Kleberg, Jr., had passed away the year before; since the number of King Ranch heirs had multiplied, a new dawn of Ranch management was emerging. The tradition of the King Ranch auctions; however, remained.

1980

Prior to the 1980 sale, SOLTERA PEPPY continued to keep the name of Mr San Peppy before the public by tying for 3rd and 4th in the 1979 NCHA Derby. MISS CHICA SAN, purchased by William B. Blakemore of Midland, Texas, and MR SAN CUATRO, purchased by GLS Farms, Inc., West Chicago, Illinois, brought $17,000 each, topping the 17 Mr San Peppy colts, helping his offspring average $10,776.47.

Peppy San Sis, a palomino yearling filly by Peppy San Badger, topped the 1980 sale, bringing $53,000 from Burnett Ranches, inc., Fort Worth, Texas. Shown with their new purchase are Mr. and Mrs. B. F. Phillips. Photo courtesy of King Ranch Archives, King Ranch, Inc.

The most important agenda for the 1980 sale, however, was the addition of the first Little Peppy colts to enter the sale ring. Although Mr San Peppy was touted as the King, whiffs of Little Peppy as a popular "Prince" fluttered over King Ranch. The atmosphere tingled with excitement when a Peppy San Badger yearling, PEPPY SAN SIS, a palomino mare, rocked the arena with her purchase price of $53,000 from Burnett Ranches, Inc., Fort

Worth, Texas. It was an easy $25,000 higher than LIL PEPPYS CUTTER, the closest high seller at $28,000. In fact, the least expensive Little Peppy offspring brought $8,000, $800 higher than the least expensive Mr San Peppy filly. King Ranch, however, while watching the popularity of its "Prince" grow, still saw him as the seed crop for Mr San Peppy.

1981 SALE

The year 1980 had been a good one for both King Ranch stallions in the show arena. Little Peppy earned the title of 1980 NCHA World Reserve Champion, adding to his own growing list of credits and, at the same time, promoting his sire.

Also, a Mr San Peppy offspring, ORGAN GRINDER, placed in the 1980 NCHA Top 10. Riding on those laurels, King Ranch continued to push Mr San Peppy and the October 10, 1981 sale catalog honored him as the foundation of the present-day King Ranch Quarter Horse program.

Once again, however, Little Peppy offspring stole the show when GLS Farms, Inc., West Chicago, Il., returned to buy LITTLE PEPPY FIVE for $52,000. J.W. McFarlane of Houston, Texas, purchased the high-selling Mr San Peppy yearling, CHANGA DE PEPPY, for $31,000. Interestingly, even though five more Mr San Peppy offspring sold than Peppy San Badger, since the

The King Ranch offered a good meal along with top sale horses. Photo courtesy King Ranch Archives, King Ranch, Inc.

younger sire's progeny brought the highest dollars, the average of the colts: $17,340 for Mr San Peppy offspring and $17,250 for Peppy San Badger offspring, differed less than $100.

Although the economy was faltering, life was just as lively in the outside world as it was at the King Ranch Sale. Americans warmed to Ronald Reagan as their new President, while the First Lady, Nancy Reagan, revitalized the style of women's dress. Then, on March 20, 1981, the nation was shocked to hear on their evening news that John W. Hinckley had shot the President.

1982 SALE

The faltering economy of 1981 continued to stress America in 1982. The *Saturday Review* magazine suspended publication after two years of losses, more than 30 banks failed and by October, 4,600,000 people were receiving unemployment compensation, the largest in history. Searching for a way to escape such reality, Americans kept the box offices hopping to see the movie "E.T.".

However, the sale of King Ranch horses showed little weakening. Mr San Peppy offspring, MISS PEPPY ALSO, highlighted her sire by winning the 1981 NCHA Super Stakes Reserve Championship and the NCHA 1981 Derby Co-Reserve Championship. TENINO SAN made another plus for the stallion by winning the 1982 NCHA World Championship.

With the October 9, 1982 Sale, Little Peppy received equal billing and shined as brightly as his sire in the King Ranch's star collection. With 17 foals sired by Mr San Peppy in the Sale, MOSCA SAN topped the Sale, purchased by H. M. Northington, Jr. of San Antonio, Texas, for $20,000. With 10 Little Peppy foals in the Sale, it was the largest offering to date. J.M. & T Enterprises of Gunnison, Colorado, took home the high-selling horse, after plunking down $62,000 for LIL ROBYNS PEP. With that purchase, Peppy San Badger yearlings averaged $16,110 while Mr San Peppy yearlings averaged $11,294.12.

1983 SALE

While little girls wanted Cabbage Patch dolls and Americans thrilled to the mini series " The Thorn Birds" and "The Winds of War," the Western world pursued its interest in King Ranch stallions. By Sale time, noted Mr San Peppy offspring TENINO SAN, with $119,812 in earnings from his World Championship, NCHA Futurity finals, Derby finals and NCHA Classic finals, was a feather in his sire's cap. In addition, MISS PEPPY ALSO had returned to win the 1982 NCHA Classic Open Reserve Championship and was the $5,000 Non-Pro Champion.

The two helped swing the pendulum of interest to Mr San Peppy for the 1983 sale, his offspring averaging $13,550. Jack Phillips of Gladewater, Texas, purchased SENOR CUATRO to top the sale with a $26,000 price tag. LAUREL PEPPY, a Little Peppy stallion purchased by Roberto Ildarraz of Argentina, brought $20,000, increasing the average of the Peppy San Badger yearlings to $9,833.33.

1984 SALE

With the economy booming again, Reagan won another election and the world slowly turned its attention toward physical fitness. Little Peppy, now 10 years old and with offspring exploding in the winning circles for the past several years, finally demanded the crown from his sire. He, instead of Mr San

Peppymint Twist, sired by Peppy San Badger, was the 1983 NCHA Derby co-champion and Champion of the 1984 NCHA 5-Year-Old Classic. Photo by Larry Graham.

Peppy, proved that King Ranch had accomplished the goal, begun with the purchase of Old Sorrel years ago, to produce offspring as good or better than their sire and dam. The number of Mr San Peppy offspring began a continual decline in King Ranch sales, while Little Peppy offspring increased.

From his first foal crop, two of the top five horses in the Open division of the 1983 NCHA Futurity were Little Peppy progeny, as were four of the top 10 in the Non-Pro division.

One of the reasons was Little Peppy offspring championships during the previous year. PEPINIC won the 1983 NCHA Non-Pro Futurity Reserve Championship while PEPPYMINT TWIST was Co-Champion of the 1983 NCHA Derby as well as the Champion of the 1984 NCHA 5-Year-Old Classic. HAIDAS LITTLE PEP snatched the title of 1983 NCHA Futurity Reserve Champion and 1984 TQHA National Stakes Champion.

Little Peppy progeny were shining in arenas other than cutting as well. PEPPYS WHIRLPOOL attested to his bloodlines in calf roping by placing 9th in the 1983 AQHA World Championship Show Jr Calf Roping class and 7th in Heeling. IM FULL OF PEP won the NRCHA World Champion Snaffle Bit Futurity.

In Mr San Peppy's court, SAN PEPPY SAM, tied for 3rd place in the 1983 Augusta Futurity, then tied for 4th place in the Tropicana Classic. The stallion, a 5-year-old and a full brother to 1982 NCHA World Champion, TENINO SAN, led the sale of 32 lots in 1984, with John R. McClelland, New Iberia, Lousiana, purchasing him for $33,000. Little Peppy yearlings averaged $17,700, boosted by the sale of TYKES LITTLE PEPPY to Gene and Helen Willingham of Vernon, Texas, for $35,000.

1985 SALE

Little Peppy offspring continued to grab the limelight. HAIDAS LITTLE PEP won the 1984 Big Country Maturity Championship while PEPPYMINT TWIST returned to claim the title of 1984 NCHA Open

Classic Champion. Also PEPPY POLKA DOT was the Big Country Non-Pro Maturity Champion.

In AQHA competition, LITTLE MARVEL earned an AQHA Superior Award in Open Cutting and also placed 4th in Open High-Point Cutting Horse competition.

Breeding to Little Peppy was hitting its peak, the pendulum slowly swinging away from Mr San Peppy foals in the cutting arena. However, Mr San Peppy's offspring, with their powerful hindquarters, were finding a niche in the roping arena. With 30 lots in the Sale, only five Mr San Peppy offspring were offered, compared to 20 Little Peppy offspring. Still, MISS SAN LENA, Mr San Peppy's high selling horse, brought $30,000 from H.M. Northington Jr. In addition, he also purchased LITTLE VIBORA SAN, the high-selling Little Peppy yearling, for $31,000. Three years earlier, Northington had also purchased Mr San Peppy's high-selling yearling. From this Sale, Little Peppy offspring averaged $12,495.

While Little Peppy was replacing Mr San Peppy, Compact Discs were replacing LP records and both were warmly received by the public. Coca Cola, however, tried to change its 99-year-old recipe but received the American cold shoulder.

1986 SALE

In the previous year, Little Peppy progeny flocked to the winner's circle in almost every show across the country. DRY SAN PRINCESS won the 1985 NCHA Non-Pro Derby Reserve Championship and the Texas Cutting Classic Derby Non-Pro Reserve Championship. PEPPY SHEA won the Tropicana Futurity Reserve Championship, while PEPPY PETITE won the 1985 NCHA Super Stakes Non-Pro Reserve Championship. TENINO BADGER claimed the 1985 National Stakes Cutting Championship for 4 year olds.

There were more: PEPPY POLKA DOC returned to win the Tropicana

Spectacular Classic Championship in both the Open and Non-Pro Divisions; HAIDAS LITTLE PEP won the Atlantic Coast Classic Reserve Championship; PEPPYMINT TWIST took two more titles as the 1985 National Stakes 6-Year-Old Champion and the 1985 NCHA Challenge Co-Reserve Championship; TOT O GIN split 3rd and 4th at the 1985 inauguaral NCHA Breeders Cup, while MR SAN DANCER won the championship titles of both the $3,000 and $1,500 Novice classes at the 1985 NCHA Area Work-offs.

In addition, PEPPYS TOAST was Reserve Champion of the Southeastern Cutting Futurity and the Atlantic Coast Futurity. MR KING PEPPY was the 1985 5-Year-Old Governor's Classic Non-Pro Champion and PEPPY PAR THREE won the Open division of the NRCHA World Championship Snaffle Bit Futurity.

With these winners writing its introduction, the 35th Annual King Ranch Sale offered 14 Little Peppy offspring, but only five Mr San Peppy offspring. This time, Mac Northington purchased PEPPYS TRANSACTION, by Mr San Peppy, to top his progeny at $10,000, while LITTLE PEPPY COKE topped the Little Peppy yearlings, bringing $26,000 from Dr. Robert McGehee.

Brothers, Scott and Tio Kleberg, at a King Ranch sale. Photo courtesy King Ranch Archives, King Ranch, Inc.

However, dark clouds had rumbled in on the American economy, with the effects reaching the King Ranch auction. The average dropped drastically for both horses, with Mr San Peppy offspring averaging $4,680 while Little Peppy offspring averaged $7,242.86. The Challenger disaster and a fluctuating economy left America somber.

1987 SALE

Mr San Peppy's offspring from the previous year's star line-up included MR. SAN MIO, a son which won the 1986 Old Fort Days Classic Championship. An entourage of Little Peppy colts also continued to increase the stallion's fame. To prime the 1987 Sale, CALS SAN BADGER won the 1986 NCHA Open Futurity Co-Reserve Championship and DELTA FLYER, a Paint stallion sired by Little Peppy, won the 1986 NCHA Super Stakes Open Championship. LIL PEPPYS BELLE won the 1986 TQHA National Stakes for 6 year olds; MISS QUIXOTE SAN won the 1986 Atlantic Coast Derby Open Reserve Championship and the West Texas Maturity Open Reserve Championship, and LITTLE SAN RITA was the 1986 Texas Cutting Classic Non-Pro Maturity Champion. HAIDAS LITTLE PEP was the NCHA Reserve World Champion and the 1986 NCHA Challenge Open Reserve Champion, while DOCS GINGER PEPPY won the 1986 California Cutting Horse Association Futurity.

In AQHA competition SOLANOS PEPPY SAN placed 10th in high point
reining and 10th in the 1986 AQHA World Show Senior Reining.

An article in the *Southern Horseman*, April 1987 issue, page 28, stated:

> "At the 1986 NCHA Futurity alone, 54 Little Peppy foals were cataloged, with 53 showing at the event, meaning that nearly eight percent of the entrants were his offspring. An impressive 37 of these get went on to the second go-round, and 15 made it to the semifinals. Eleven Little Peppy offspring went all the way to the finals, six in the Open division and five in the Non-Pro.

> "Translated into total numbers and earnings, 207 stallions represented the 703 entries in the 1986 Futurity. When it was over, the 11 finalists by Little Peppy had earned $308,154, which was about 27 percent of the $1,128,060 purse. Overall, in aged-event competition for 3, 4, 5 and 6-year-olds in 1986, Little Peppy was the second-leading sire. His offspring earned a whopping $1,102,553."

Of the 31 lots offered to the public at the 1987 auction, only two of them were Mr San Peppy offspring, but they both sold well. CAMISETA SAN topped his colts, selling to Reidy Land & Cattle Co. for $15,000, helping Mr San Peppy offspring to average $11,000. Over in the Little Peppy camp, 16 Little Peppy offspring sold. PAR PEPPY, bought by Northington Ranches, brought $25,000 to top the Sale, helping Little Peppy offspring average $9,006.67.

That same year, the emotional tide over the Vietnam War surfaced in movies such as "Full Metal Jacket" and "Good Morning Vietnam." Fred Astaire died; Sam Walton was named the world's richest man for the third year, while on October 19, one of the greatest stock market crashes in history changed the financial status of many other Americans.

Cals San Badger, sired by Peppy San Badger and ridden by Pat Earnheart, was Co-Reserve Champion of the 1986 NCHA Open Futurity. Photo by Pat Hall.

REMUDA SALES

In the late 1980's, the American economy continued to sag heavily and by 1990, unemployment was at its highest since mid-1987. Ten of America's largest industries laid off 161,000 workers, postage stamps increased from 25 cents to 29 cents and King Ranch offered several Remuda Sales to the public. One such sale, held May 27-28, 1988, offered 358 horses for sale; 66 of those were horses of all ages sired by Little Peppy. In May 1989, a two-day sale offered 297 head to the public.

Little Peppy offspring had captured their share of the 1987 winner's circles, helping to entice buyers to come to the Sale. DELTA FLYER was Co-Reserve Champion of the Tropicana Hotel Cutting Spectacular; CD CHICA SAN BADGER executed a double championship, winning both the Open and the Non-Pro division of the 1987 National Stakes Derby as well as the Augusta Derby Non-Pro Championship; LILS PEPPY LENA won the 1987 Augusta Open Derby; MISS MARMOSET was the 1987 NCHA Super Stakes Non-Pro Reserve Champion and POWDER RIVER PLAYBOY was the 1987 Bonanza Cutting Champion.

Little Peppy offspring had won $419,619 in the1988 NCHA Futurity, taking home 28 percent of the total purse in the Open and Non-Pro divisions. He was also the top money-winning sire of all 140 stallions represented, with 25 percent of the top 60 horses, in both Open and Non-Pro competition, being sired by him. A total of 35 percent of all Little Peppy offspring entered in the Futurity, finishing in the money. (*Quarter Horse News*)

CD Chica San Badger, a daughter of Peppy San Badger, won both the Open and Non-Pro divisions of the 1987 TQHA National Stakes Derby as well as the Augusta Derby Non-Pro title. Photo by Pat Hall.

LIL PEPPY LYNX won the Big Country Non-Pro Cutting Futurity; LYNX AND PEPPY won the 1988 El Cid Classic; MARVILLA PEP won the Non-Pro division of the Heart Of Oklahoma Cutting Futurity; QUAKETTA won the Non-Pro division of the TQHA 4-Year-Old Aged event; BADGERS DRY won the 1988 Oregon Cutting Futurity, and GAJES BRANDO won the Non-Pro division of the Northwest Cutting Classic.

Little Peppy offspring, competing in 1988, won over $1,346,469, according to **Equi Stat**, a division of *Quarter Horse News*. The total included all aged-event results plus all NCHA-approved cuttings.

DOX HAPPY TIMES, sired by Little Peppy, won the Non-Pro division of the 1989 Las Vegas Derby; PEPPYS STAR RIO had won the 1989 Super Stakes; CLAYS LITTLE PEPPY had won the 1989 Memphis Open Championship, the NCHA Breeders Open Championship and the Super Stakes Reserve Championship title; IMARI TARI won the 1989 NCHA Open Super Stakes Classic

Powder River Playboy, a son of Peppy San Badger ridden by Greg Welch, was the 1987 Bonanza Cutting Champion. Photo by Fred Miller.

and the 1988 Augusta Open Futurity Championship; MISS PEPPY LENA was the 1989 NCHA Super Stakes Non-Pro Reserve Champion and BADGER SAN DOC was the 1989 Bonanza Non-Pro Champion and the NCHA Super Stakes Reserve Champion.

In AQHA competition, IRON BADGER MISS was the High-Point earner in AQHA Open Cutting while IRISH SAN BADGER won the AQHA Amateur Reserve Champion Reining Horse title in 1989. LITTLE DRY SAN was the 1989 AQHA Reserve Champion Jr Working Cow Horse; MR SAN BADGER DOC was AQHA Reserve Champion High-Point Team Penning in Youth competition and PEPPY BADGER CHEX won the 1989 World Champion Open Jr. Reining Horse title.

An advertisement in the Sept, 8, 1989, *Quarter Horse News*, referring to

Little Peppy, stated that 42 of his offspring had won $529,481 in the Augusta Futurity, the Bonanza and the NCHA Super Stakes. The list included 30 4-year-olds and 11 5-year-olds. Six of those horses earned money in all three events. Little Peppy offspring took the first five places in the NCHA Super Stakes, as well as 8th place. In 1989, Little Peppy topped the list of sires, with foals by him winning $1,809,154.

In 1990, BADGERS CANDY MAN won the Missouri Cutting Maturity; BR PEPPY DOC won the Amateur division of the Reno Western Futurity; DUAL PEP was the Non-Pro champion of the Bonanza Classic, the PCCHA 5/6-Year-Old Open Champion and the NCHA Classic Open and Non-Pro Champion.

POP A TOP PEP won the 1990 Augusta Futurity; RUM SQUALL was the 1990 PCCHA Derby Reserve Champion; DOCS PEPPY GEM won the NCHA Super Stakes and OKAY PEPPY was Reserve Champion of the Memphis Classic.

In 1990, Little Peppy led the way, being the leading sire in the cutting industry for the third year. According to **Equi Stat**, a division of *Quarter Horse News*, his get, in all-ages, all-divisions, had won $1,759,801. Offspring led three of the four charts when broken down by foal years. King Ranch was also the top breeder in all ages, all divisions, with horses bred by them winning $424,331.

1991

July 26, 1991, ushered in an auction with a new format and a new trend as King Ranch joined hands with Atwood Ranches to host the "Best of the 90's" Production Sale held during the NCHA Summer Spectacular in Fort Worth, Texas. From the 20 King Ranch offspring offered for sale, 15 were Little Peppy colts and the stage for their sale was still being set by prior-year champions. At the auction, Jerry Roberts purchased TACHITAS LAST for $43,000 to top the Sale and the average for Little Peppy colts was $11,813.33.

1992 SALE

The next year, the Sale held July 31, 1992, was a repeat of the year before. Atwood and King Ranch teamed up for a Second Annual Production Sale in Fort Worth in which King Ranch offered 25 lots to the public. Keeping the Little Peppy name before the public, PEPPYS DOCS MIMOSA won 1991 Augusta Futurity; PEPPYS TACHITA had taken home the "gold" at the 1991 NCHA Breeders Cup; PEPPYS FROM HEAVEN was the 1991 NCHA Derby Non-Pro Champion AND BADGER SAN DOC won the Non-Pro division of the Southern Cutting Futurity.

In AQHA competition, LITTLE QUINTO was the 1991 Youth Reserve Champion in High-Point Team Penning; SAN BADGER CHEX placed 8th in the AQHA High-Point Senior Working Cow Horse standings; IRISH SAN BADGER was 1991 Reserve World Champion Reining Horse and PEPPY PACITO won the World Championship in Team Penning,

1993 SALE

While still being partners, Atwood and King Ranch changed the date of the sale to December so it could be held during the NCHA Futurity. Also, during that year, LITTLE QUINTO placed sixth at the AQHA Youth World Show in Team Penning; POCO PEPPY LYNX was Reserve Champion in AQHA High-Point Reining; TANG N PEP was awarded second in High-Point Senior Cutting as well as taking the World Championship in Senior Cutting and TEJONS LITTLE LENA finished third in AQHA Senior Working Cow Horse.

In NCHA aged events, CERRADA BADGE won the Meadow Vue 4-Year-Old Futurity; CHIP AWAY PEPPY won the 1992 El Cid Futurity; LIL SAN BENITO was the Non-Pro Champion of the Biggest Little Futurity 5/6-Year-Old Division; JUST SWINGIN PEPPY captured the 1992 Augusta Futurity Open Reserve Championship and COMMANDO PEPPY won the Northwest Cutting Derby.

COOL AND PEPPY won the Non-Pro division of the Texas Gold 5/6-Year-Old; LITTLE BADGER DULCE was the 1992 NCHA Futurity Reserve Champion and LITTLE TENINA was Reserve Champion of the Montgomery Cutting Futurity and Champion of the 1992 NCHA Derby. AMANDO PEPPY took his rider to the 1992 NCHA Non-Pro World Championship.

Topping the 1993 Sale, Marilyn Jo Franz purchased TINAS BARS PEPPY for $23,000. The 13 offspring averaged $8,911.54.

1994 SALE

The last joint endeavor of the Atwood and King Ranches returned once again to the summer months and the NCHA Summer Spectacular. There, 12 King Ranch colts by Little Peppy and four by Mr San Peppy sold. Atwood, however, had 13 of its own Little Peppy offspring in the Sale. The highest-selling King Ranch offspring, RETSINA BADGER, was purchased by Ronald Wheeler of Turlock, California, for $16,200.00 and the average of Little Peppy foals was $5,700.

To help keep prices up, Little Peppy offspring were still winning. LITTLE BADGER DULCE had won the 1993 NCHA Super Stakes Open Championship, the 1993 Bonanza and then won the 1995 NCHA Reserve World Championship title. CLEMGILS BESS won the PCCHA Amateur Derby and PEPPYS BO DIDDLY was Co-Reserve Champion of the Non-Pro Division of the NCHA Super Stakes..

If one looked at all the cutting horse sales for that year, they would find that 78 Little Peppy colts sold, averaging $11,229 and grossing $885,850, making him the leading sire of offspring selling in 1993. It happened again in 1994, when 64 head were sold, averaging $12,967, grossing $829,9001 Once again, Little Peppy led as the number one sire of highest-selling horses.

Although 1994 ended the prestigious auctions, the legend still lives on.

OMLENA PEPPY won the 1994 AQHA Youth Reining Reserve World Championship as well as the Reserve World Championship in Working Cow Horse; LIL PEP O LENA won the Souther Cutting Futurity; HEMANO SAN won the Gum Tree Amateur Futurity and CEASAR O LENA won the All-American Amateur Tournament.

LITTLE REY DOC was the 1995 AQHA Reserve World Champion Amateur Cutter; TARIS LITTLE VINTAGE was the 1995 AQHA World Champion Junior Reining Horse and PEPPYS RED LACE won the 1994 Abilene 4-Year-Old Spectacular Non-Pro Division.

MR SAN OLEN was the 1992 NRCHA Futurity Open Champion; PEPTOBOONSMAL won the 1995 NCHA Futurity, then continued on to collect first at the Gold Coast and the 1996 Bonanza; GOT PEP won the 1995 Montana CHA Futurity and BABE LEANA BADGER won the 1996 Chisholm Trail Derby.

These, however, only represent a random representation of the horses sired by Little Peppy which placed in the performance arena. The records of the accomplishments of Little Peppy offspring would be a book within itself.

20

The Latter years

G row old with me;
The best is yet to be -
The last of life for which the first was made.
Robert Browning

L ife amazingly disguises its ability to quietly erode the vigor of
youth. In one's "prime," only rarely do fleeting thoughts concede
that the sunset days grow closer every hour. Even when vigor
loses its luster, thus forcing that reality, it isn't easy to accept, since the
acceptance is not just of the physical demise. It is also the mental yearning
for what once was, for yesterday's springtime that has changed to autumn.
So it was with Little Peppy.

"It was all over but the shouting," reminisced Dr. Toelkes, who was moving the King Ranch stallions away from the Ranch. Since at times such talk seemed almost like treason, it was a decision that had not come easily, but one that had been discussed over the last two years until it was threadbare. Any more discussing would not improve the situation or make the move any easier. Little Peppy had been good to all of them, and in the good years, it had been easy to forget that all things come to an end.

"In 1985 and 1986, his productivity was at his maximum. By 1992, we were in a 45-60 percent decline," explained Toelkes. "We still bred a mare every other day while she was in heat, but by 1992, we were only getting two million live sperm in her 95 percent of the time. Optimally, you want five million. I had experienced decline with Mr San Peppy when he was 16 or 17 also, so I wasn't all that surprised."

Toelkes hunted remedies to stall the continual decline and finally received some success with Dr. Bill Pickett at Colorado State University. Having taken several reproduction seminars from Dr. Pickett and knowing that his team did semen evaluations all over the world, Toelkes called him to discuss Little Peppy. Dr. Pickett and Dr. Kirk Shiner, a veterinarian who had moved to Colorado from Lexington, Kentucky, to team with Pickett, visited King Ranch in October 1992.

"They completely went over the horse," described Toelkes. "They did serial blood samples and sent them to Colorado State University for analysis. They collected him at intervals to determine his semen productions, measuring his hormone levels. He was checked from bottom to top. They thought if we gave him GNRH in pulse-like doses, maybe we could slow down the testicular degeneration. We tried doing this on a regular basis and it was okay for awhile, but then we needed to give it to him around the clock, so they developed a pump system and put a catheter under his skin."

Still, this did not solve the commercial breeding program dilemma on King Ranch. Toelkes believed it was time to move Little Peppy. He and

Paul Studnicka together went to Tio's office to finalize their on-going conversation. Tio, who knew closing the commercial breeding facilities was inevitable, had left the timing of that call in Toelkes' hands.

"At that point, we had a number of customers who had bred mares with us for a lot of years. Toelkes had determined that we could only breed 'x' number of mares to Little Peppy and that meant King Ranch needed to reduce the number of mares we bred to him. If we were going to reduce our mares, then it made sense to close our doors and make him more accessible to the public," said Tio.

The reasons for the move outweighed any consideration for continuing the present commercial breeding program at King Ranch. Although the stallion had been extremely fertile, easily breeding more than 200 mares for numerous years, he was no longer able to do so. If large numbers of King Ranch mares could not be bred, then standing Little Peppy in a more central location was more advantageous for mare owners. In addition, with Little Peppy's semen count fragile, for every King Ranch mare that was bred, an outside breeding fee was lost. With an economy down, the colts' prices were not what they had been during the oil-booming 80's and often a $6,000 breeding fee was more than a colt brought in a sale. Keeping the breeding facility open for only one horse left more minuses than pluses on the balance sheet.

"While Little Peppy still bred a lot of mares," stated Toelkes, "there weren't that many mares being bred to Mr San Peppy or to Dry Doc, so he was supporting the entire breeding program. He was mainly paying all the salaries, buying the feed, supporting the advertising and the behind-the-scenes book work. There was no profit in that. It made more sense to place him at a breeding farm where once again several stallions paid the expenses. Also, there was just the matter of promoting 'good will.' When we took a colt off of King Ranch to another sale, it was like we were in competition with ourselves. By then, all of the Little Peppy offspring had babies, like the Haidas Little Peps and the Dual Peps. I went to a sale in Fort Worth in which there were 60-plus horses; 49 of them were by Little Peppy or his sons."

All of the reasons pointed toward better breeding for Little Peppy and better economic conditions for King Ranch if they closed the commercial breeding program. Tio called Joe Stiles.

"I told Joe to find the best place available for both of the stallions. He made the decision to place Mr San Peppy at the Lazy E in Guthrie, Oklahoma, and to place Little Peppy at Bullard Farms in Weatherford, Texas, a closer arrangement for cutting-horse mares," said Tio.

Little Peppy while he was at Bullard's Breeding Farm in Weatherford, Texas. Photo courtesy King Ranch Archives, King Ranch, Inc.

Before the move was over, making the decision because of economic sense proved easier than accepting it emotionally. The lives of Little Peppy and Mr San Peppy had intertwined with the lives of the people of King Ranch for 16 years; they had brought to King Ranch excitement, activity and fame. Closing the doors to that business was unlike closing the doors of any other business. When other doors closed, employees walked away and were no longer daily reminded of the severing of the umbilical cord.

At King Ranch, however, the people lived where they worked, so daily they saw the empty stallion barn, the deserted paddocks and the uninhabited mare stalls at the Creek Barn. Unable to walk away from the closed business, its remnants acted as a daily reminder of what once was, thus making the grieving process that accompanies all major changes slow to heal.

"The Lazy E people came down and picked up Mr San Peppy," remembered Knudsen. "It was really emotional. I hated to see the horses go. Since Mr San Peppy and I came at the same time, that one really got me. I loaded him in the trailer, shut the door on him, then just stood there while they drove off with him."

"It was a sad day for all of us," agreed Janell Kleberg. "Like the ancient Sythians that roamed Europe on fine horses 700 years before Christ, then vanished; that whole civilization that revolved around those stallions seemed to vanish overnight.

"The Creek Barn is eerily silent now," she continued. "Now, our gratification comes, not from being a part of the breeding of those stallions, but from all of the good horses under saddle working on these ranches that were born from them in those paddocks across the creek."

For the next few years, neither stallion came home, staying year around at their breeding facilities. Several of those from the Ranch went to visit them,

Mr San Peppy, shown at age 25, at the Lazy E Ranch in Guthrie, Okla. Photo courtesy of King Ranch Archives, King Ranch, Inc.

however, and in January 1993, while Little Peppy stood at Bullards, Dr. Toelkes made a trip himself, his third one to Texas A & M because of an impaction in Little Peppy.

"They opened him up and massaged it," remembered Toelkes and he did just fine. As soon as he was able, he returned to Bullard's to convalesce rather than back down here."

With a shake of his head, Toelkes laughed as he compared the health of Little Peppy to that of his sire, Mr San Peppy. "While we had these problems with Little Peppy, Mr San Peppy was absolutely made our of iron. In fact, I went to see him once at the Laze E and he was hog fat. They told me they'd cut back his rations but he was still fat. The minute I looked into his stall, I knew why. He was standing on wheat straw and he'd never seen that before he went up there, so he was continually eating his bedding."

COMING HOME

At first, King Ranch sent a limited number of mares to be bred to Little Peppy while he stood at Bullard Farms. With each passing year, however, as Little Peppy's breeding power diminished, King Ranch stopped breeding any mares to him.

"We made that decision after we sent about 15 mares up there and Dr. Bullard called to say he was having trouble getting all of the mares bred," said Tio. "Our answer was to breed the customers' mares, first; only after they are all bred, if possible, breed ours.' After that year, we did not send any more of our mares."

In the spring of 1996, four years after Little Peppy left King Ranch, Dr. Bullard called Dr. Toelkes on several occasions to discuss the difficulty of breeding Little Peppy. "I'd been up there in February," recalled Toelkes. "At that time, he had not been collected yet. Between March 1 and April 1, though, he inseminated 11 mares, but none of them settled. His semen was looking worse all the time."

While the decision to move the stallions away from King Ranch had been difficult to make, Mother Nature made the decision to return them to the Ranch easy. Before spring turned to summer, Little Peppy came home. Mr San Peppy had already arrived two seasons earlier.

RETIREMENT

Now, each morning, Paul Studnicka, with halter in hand, walks to the paddock where Little Peppy lives, about half the length of a football field from Studnicka's office in the Creek Barn. The stallion, now familiar with his retirement routine, waits expectantly for his old friend to take him to a stall where he will eat his morning feed. After Little Peppy is safely behind the latched door, Studnicka returns to another paddock to retrieve Mr San Peppy and place him in a stall for his morning feeding.

"After they're settled and eating, we then do a few other chores," reflected Studnicka, of the daily routine with the retired famous stallions. "We work the baby calves, feed the other horses or just do barn jobs, giving them time to eat."

After breakfast, however, it's time to "dress" for the day. Emeterio Silguero bathes the horses several times a week, meticulously brushing them on the days in between, shining their coats for the tourists who come daily to see them. By 9:30 a.m., Little Peppy and Mr San Peppy are back in their paddocks ready for visitors. Tour buses, leaving hourly from the King Ranch Visitor Center, travel the back roads of the vast Ranch, visiting points of interest, telling the story of Captain King's legacy. One of those stops is alongside the paddocks of Peppy and Little Peppy for viewing of the King Ranch legends.

"It's a relief to have Little Peppy home and in good health so he can live out his life in the pasture next to the Creek Barn," remarked Janell. "Emeterio pampers him just as he did during all of those breeding seasons. The relationship between the men and horses here is tangible; you can sense it. In addition to all that petting, busloads of visitors stop by to give him the adulation that he richly deserves."

The proof of the pampering from Paul Studnicka and Emeterio was revealed last spring when Janell started to take pictures of the stallions. "I wanted to take pictures of Mr San Peppy in the tall grass," she smiled. "But Emeterio told me, 'Oh, he only walks where it is mowed.' "

LINE BREEDING: FROM OLD SORREL TO LITTLE PEPPY

E*very once in a while it clicks. A stallion comes along that sets the equine world on fire with his talent and then passes his ability on to his progeny. The difficulty arises in perpetuating that talent generation after generation. In the early 1900's, a young Bob Kleberg found an exceptionally good looking yearling among the offspring of George Clegg's "wax dolls," his name for the 20 broodmares he had selectively accumulated. In a letter to Bob Denhart, author of* **King Ranch Quarter Horses***, Bob Kleberg wrote about himself:*

"At that time, I had no authority to buy anything for the Ranch; so I went to my cousin Caesar, who did have this authority, and asked him if he would not go over and inspect these mares and foals and try to buy one to five colts, especially one chestnut colt which I thought was by far the best of the lot. Caesar did this very soon after I mentioned it. When he saw the sorrel foal, he was impressed just as I was. He asked George Clegg what he would take for a foal like that, pointing

205

to the sorrel foal. George said he would take $125.00. Caesar said he would buy
the foal. George then said he did not want to sell that one. Caesar told him that
he had asked specifically, and he had said 'that one.' Caesar said he wanted him
delivered and, of course, he was."

Accdording to Kleberg in his letter, the colt, named Old Sorrel, sired by Hickory Bill, a son of Peter McCue, was purchased expressly to improve the blood of the King Ranch horses, as they had tried to do with other stallions in the past. Kleberg broke and trained Old Sorrel himself

"Old Sorrel did everything," said Helen Groves. "Daddy rode on him, cut on him, roped on him and raced him. Mother was a hunter and also loved horses and riding, so Daddy built her a corral to train horses for riding and jumping. My mother and father were arguing once about whether a horse had to be a Thoroughbred to jump well, so Daddy got Tio's father, who had done some jumping while in school in Virginia, to jump Old Sorrel. The two cleared the four-foot bars without even a problem in the hitchcock corral, with him riding bareback and using a halter. That convinced my mother that there were some horses that could jump as high as Thoroughbreds."

As the story was told by Bob Gray in **Horseman** magazine in January 1966, Mrs. Kleberg, visibly impressed, asked her husband, "How did you know he would jump?"

"Well," explained the King Ranch boss, "he'll sure jump prickly pear and mesquite. No reason why he wouldn't jump these."

Stories like these embrace the life of Old Sorrel. The exceptional stallion, intelligent, quick and nimble, was also filled with faith in his master, Bob Kleberg.

"There was a place, where bachelors retired from the Ranch, that had a set of steep stairs leading to a dining room upstairs. The ceilings were probably 25 to 30 feet tall. Daddy took Old Sorrel up and down those stairs

206

one time, just to prove that he could do it," said Helen.

While Old Sorrel daily affirmed he was the kind of cow horse King Ranch needed for cattle work, the Ranch was busy introducing a new breed of cattle, the Santa Gertrudis, using the somewhat controversial breeding method of linebreeding. Crossing a bull named Monkey, the product of crossbreeding Brahman with Shorthorn, on first-cross heifers and then on

Old Sorrel in March of 1943 at age 28. Photo courtesy King Ranch Archives, King Ranch, Inc,

second-cross heifers, they created a foundation gene pool. Monkey's sons were then mated to his daughters and other sons to granddaughters until every animal in the program was descended from that single superior individual.

Using this line breeding program, King Ranch developed a foundation gene pool that continually created superior animals, generation after generation. Bob Kleberg, realizing that type of breeding passed on quality

207

genes, began experimenting with line breeding in their Quarter Horse program. He used his favorite horse, Old Sorrel, as the designer pattern.

"Daddy, he loved challenges and this looked like a new one," continued Helen. "He was a voracious reader and read scientific journals on heredity all of the time. Since he was especially fond of Old Sorrel, he used his sons and grandsons and breed those horses back and forth, keeping that blood. You had to know your horses to do it, but Daddy did and he knew which ones would go with which families."

OLD SORREL LINEAGE

The Ranch aim, to preserve the blood of Old Sorrel, dedicated a host of great sons by Old Sorrel to this purpose: Solis, Macanudo, Babe Grande, Little Richard, Cardinal and Hired Hand, which was sired by the stallion when he was 30 years old. These sons were bred to each other's daughters and granddaughters to perpetuate the Old Sorrel bloodline. Both Macanudo and Little Richard are in the pedigree of Little Peppy.

Offspring of Old Sorrel include (from left) grandsons Wimpy and Peppy, and sons Macanudo and Babe Grande. Photo courtesy King Ranch Archives, King Ranch, Inc.

Stallions such as Pep-Up, Peppy and Wimpy became stars in the second generation. "Flour used to come in cloth sacks and Peppy was pictured on some flour sacks at one time," remembered Helen.

Pep-Up was sired by Macanudo by Old Sorrel and out of Petra R2 by Little Richard by Old Sorrel. Pep-Up, in turn, sired Peppy Belle, the dam of

208

Mr San Peppy, the sire of Little Peppy.

"Some pedigrees will show that Pep-Up was a son of Peppy P212 and out of Canalita," stated pedigree analyst Larry Thornton. This is an error that was later corrected; the sire of Pep-up is Macanudo and his dam was Petra R2. Pep-Up gives us an example of a son of Old Sorrel crossed on a granddaughter of Old Sorrel, the type of cross the King Ranch found successful in its early line breeding program to Old Sorrel.

LITTLE PEPPY'S GENEALOGY

Little Peppy, born 29 years after the death of Old Sorrel, is a sixth-generation offspring of the stallion. Although he was not inbred or line bred within the standard four or five generations of his pedigree, he does have multiple links to the great stallion Peter McCue. Peter McCue, the grandsire of Old Sorrel, appears at least 12 times in the pedigree of Peppy San Badger. Those 12 crosses provide 12 accesses for restoring in Little Peppy the foundation bloodline of Old Sorrel. Pedigree analyst Larry Thornton explains it best.

"In a discussion of Little Peppy's pedigree, we see that he has 12 crosses to Peter McCue. This is a percent of blood of 7.421875. I will cite Jay Pumphrey by stating that Jay has told me that any percent of blood over 3% will have an influence to some degree on the pedigree.

"I agree with this assessment but I will carry the significance of this breeding pattern one step farther. The fact that Little Peppy has 12 crosses to Peter McCue makes him a member of the Peter McCue family of Quarter horses. When we establish that a stallion or mare comes from a given family of horses, then we can think in terms of his genes that are passed down from the foundation sire of that family to the horse we're studying, in this case Peter McCue to Little Peppy. The more crosses found in the pedigree from that foundation sire, the more opportunities or avenues the genes can travel from the foundation sire to the horse being studied. We often hear geneticists refer to a gene pool. This pattern gives Peppy San

Badger 12 crosses to the main gene pool of Peter McCue."

PROVEN ABILITY

Little Peppy acquires his ability, to not only shine in the arena but to produce offspring that shine as well. This special ability appears to come from both sides of his pedigree. His paternal grandsire and great grandsire were Leo San and Leo. Both of these great stallions were noted for their prepotency as sires leaving a great legacy in the Quarter Horse.

Another key to his special ability can be found in the female side of his pedigree. "Some breeders theorize that the mare is 70-80 percent responsible for how the foal turns out," continued Thornton. "Some breeders live by the philosophy that 'great sires have great mothers.' If this is the case, then Peppy San Badger has two very significant mares in his pedigree: his dam, Sugar Badger, and his paternal grand dam Peppy Belle, both proven producers."

Mr San Peppy. Photo Courtesy King Ranch Archives, King Ranch, Inc.

Thornton cites Gordon Howell, the breeder of Mr San Peppy, to make his point on the kind of pedigree strength found throughout Peppy San Badger's pedigree.

"Howell had this to say about Peppy Belle and Leo San in an article by David Gaines, 'Peppy San/Mr San Peppy,' published in the July 1978 *Horseman* magazine. 'They picked up their ability as handling horses and using horses from Leo San, and they picked up their tenaciousness, that's the word tenaciousness, the ability to stay with a cow, the ability to learn and be trained to do whatever a man wants, from the dam (Peppy Belle).' Peppy San Badger's pedigree is filled from top to bottom with great individuals serving as suppliers of his genes, the kind of genes that made him the premier sire."

THE BOTTOM LINE

As Dick Kleberg once expressed to his son, Tio, "Trying to find a good stud is hard; trying to raise one is harder and raising a damned good one is near impossible" Yet, for over a century, King Ranch has been proving the near impossible is but a challenge for each new generation. Following the fame of the Old Sorrel lineage and the era of Bob Kleberg, Jr., and Dick Kleberg, Jr., their children and grandchildren picked up the torch of the King Ranch Quarter Horse program and relit it with the fame of Peppy San Badger.

Peppy San Badger with Emeterio Silguero. Photo by Janell Kleberg.

The barns now stand empty, but the echos of past champions remain, possibly to be muffled by another generation which may one day rise to once again relight the torch. Until then, the charisma and mystique of King Ranch will never fade. To the outside world, King Ranch, famous for its cattle and horses as well as its regal beauty, oddly born of desolation and allurement, are the ingredients of which dreams are made.

EPILOGUE

THE LAST LITTLE PEPPY RUNNING W

O ne of the most important tools of ranching is the horse. The working cowboy can not keep an ill-tempered horse, one that lacks intelligence or is not physical enough to get his job done. That's why it gives me great satisfaction to see the P Bar brand of Little Peppy on the hips of most of the horses under saddle here.

So long as horses continue to be used the way they are used here, with the fundamentals of good horsemanship and animal husbandry, then there will always be a breeding program to bring the best genetics together. As long as you continue to breed the best and ride the best, and use them in everyday work, you'll someday create a genetic pool that will produce another Little Peppy.

Janell Kleberg

S he looks a lot like her daddy. A blaze flows down her face and four white socks climb from her hooves a short distance upward, their brightness emphasizing her lanky legs, a characteristic of her youth. Inquisitively, the yearling peeks from behind her mother's hip, her eyes big and bright, attesting to the intelligence behind them. A regal stature about her proclaims her blue blood.

She is Pepsina.

Her dam, Doc's Retsina, a 1974 model by Doc Bar and out of Jandon, a Thoroughbred mare, has her own AQHA open show record with 11 points in Hunter Under Saddle.

She has also foaled seven other colts, such as Doc's Bo Derek, which has won $55,083; Robert Oak, with $26,032 in earnings, and

Retsina, an own daughter of Doc Bar, with her 1995 foal, Pepsina. She is the last offspring to carry the Running W brand. Photo courtesy of Paul and Jonell Studnicka.

Pepsina, the last Little Peppy offspring to wear   Running W brand. Photo courtesy of Paul and Jonell Studnicka.

Smart Lass, winner of $23,278. Money won by all of her offspring total $117,634.00 in the cutting arena.

She is also a full sister to Doc's Mahogany, the sire of Ms Royal Mahogany, the Champion of the 1980 NCHA Futurity.

Pepsina's sire is the legendary Peppy San Badger.

"If you were going to pick a Little Peppy, this is the kind you would want," described Bernie Kirkland, breeder of the yearling owned by Paul and Jonell Studnicka. "She's so elegant looking. She's good minded, real alert and quick, one that will have a lot of moves. She seems to have it all."

She has more. Pepsina carries the last Running W brand placed on a Little Peppy offspring, the last gift from the legend to the legacy.

The Little Peppy brand. Photo by Janell Kleberg.

KING RANCH CUTTERS

Tio Kleberg riding Peppys Taquito.

Leslie Clement riding Bonnie San Peppy.

Janell Kleberg riding Peppys Little Gem.

KING RANCH CUTTERS

Photo courtesy Quarter Horse News.

Helen K. Groves riding Haidas Lorri.

Photo by Teresa Jett

Caroline Alexander, showing her cutting horse at the NCHA Super Stakes.

Photo by Dalco

Martin Clement showing his cutting horse.

APPENDIX

FOR THE RECORD

During the 17 years of breeding Little Peppy (1979-1996), 2,296 foals were registered with him as their sire with the American Quarter Horse Association. He first bred mares at the age of four, then retired from the stud farm at the age of 21. His progeny, however, throughout those years, attacked the competitve arena with vigor, bringing home championship after championship, bestowing honor upon their sire along the way. The following horses are merely examples of the great horses that Little Peppy sires and by no means is a list of every horse sired by him who did well.

THE TOP 25 GET OF LITTLE PEPPY

Using information compiled by Equi-stat, a division of the *Quarter Horse News*, and the National Cutting Horse Association, the following progeny of Little Peppy were listed as the top 25 horses according to earnings as of August 1, 1996. Equi-Stat records do not include NCHA week-end show earnings from Jan. 1-Aug. 1, 1996. While many of these horses are now retired, several are still in the show arena, continually adding to their earnings record. These accomplishments are only part of their distinguished records.

1. Little Badger Dulce -
  a. lifetime earnings $555,493..
  b. 1992 NCHA Futurity Reserve Champion.
  c. 1993 Bonanza Champion.
  d. 1993 NCHA Super Stakes Champion.
  e. 1993 Steamboat Springs Derby Champion.
  f. 1994 NCHA Super Stakes Classic Champion.
  g. 1994 Steamboat Springs Derby Champion.
  h. 1995 Augusta Futurity Classic Champion.
  I. 1995 NCHA Super Stakes Classic Reserve Champion.
  j. 1995 NCHA Reserve World Champion.

2. Haidas Little Pep
  a. lifetime earnings of $425,174.
  b. 1983 NCHA Futurity Reserve Champion.
  c. Texas QHA National States Champion.
  d. Reserve Champion NCHA Classic Challenge.

3. LITTLE TENINA
  a. lifetime earnings of $394,315.
  b. 1991 Futurity Champion.
  c. Montgomery Futurity Reserve Champion.
  d. Co-Champion 1992 NCHA Derby.
  e. 1993 Abilene Spectacular Champion.
  f. Bonanza Classic Champion.

4. DUAL PEP
  a. lifetime earnings of $307,384.
  b. 1989 Bonanza Cutting Champion.

  c. NCHA Super Stakes finalist.
  d. Memphis Futurity Co-Reserve Champion.
  e. Memphis Classic/Challenge Reserve Champion.
  f. Memphis Classic/Challenge NP Res Champ.
  g. NCHA Breeders Cutting Reserve Champion.

5. CD CHICA SAN BADGER
  a. lifetime earnings of $279,038.
  b. 1986 NCHA Futurity Open finalist
  c. 1986 NCHA Futurity Non-Pro finalist
  d. 1987 Augusta Non Pro Futurity Champion.
  e. Bonanaza Non Pro champion.
  f. 1988 Reserve Champion Bonanza Classic/Challenge.

6. OKAY PEPPY
  a. lifetime earnings of $260,082.
  b. NCHA Futurity finalist.
  c. 1990 Memphis Futurity Reserve Champion.
  d. 1991 Memphis 4-Y-O Reserve Champion.
  e. 1992 Montgomery Cutting Classic Champion.

7. DELTA FLYER
  a. lifetime earnings of $259,755.
  b. 1986 Super Stakes Champion.
  c. 1988 Bonanza 5/6 year Old Champion.

8. IMARI TARI
  a. lifetime earnings of $253,188.
  b. 1988 Augusta Futurity Champion.
  c. Bonanza Reserve Champion.
  d. 1984 Non Pro Memphis Classic Champion

e.   Co-Champion of NCHA Super Stakes.

9. PEPPYMINT TWIST
a.   lifetime earnings of $215,419.
b.   1983 Augusta Futurity Champion.
c.   NCHA Derby Champion.
d.   1984 NCHA Classic Champion.
e.   1985 NCHA Challenge Co-Reserve Champion.

10. CLAYS LITTLE PEP
a.   lifetime earnings of $204,880.
b.   1989 Memphis Futurity Champion
c.   1989 NCHA Super States Reserve Champion
d.   NCHA Breeders Cutting Champion
e.   1991 Augusta Classic/Challenge Champion

11. PEPPY PLAYMATE
a.   lifetime earnings of $195,868.
b.   1983 NCHA Futurity finalist.
c.   1984 Bonanza Co Champion.
d.   NCHA Super Stakes finalist.
e.   NCHA Derby finalist.

12. AMANDO PEPPY
a.   lifetime earning of $194,824.
b.   1992 NCHA Non Pro World Champion
c.   1996 NCHA Western Work-Offs Reserve Champion Gelding.

13. PEPPY POLKA DOC
a.   lifetime earnings of $192,795.
b.   Bonanza Classic Champion.
c.   TQHA National Stakes Champion.

14. PEPPYS TACHITA
a.   lifetime earnings of $191,053.
b.   1990 Open Super Stakes finalist.
c.   1989 The Non Pro Champion.
d.   NCHA Classic/Challenge Non Pro finalist.
e.   1990 Non Pro Classic/ Challenge Champion.
f.   NCHA Breeders NP Classic / Challenge Champ.

15. LIL PEPPYS BELLE
a.   lifetime earnings of $187,364.
b.   1984 Bonanza finalist.
c.   NCHA Super Stakes finalist.
d.   tied for 4th NCHA Derby.
e.   1986 NCHA World Champion finalist.
f.   The Non Pro Champion.

16. BADGER SAN DOC
a.   lifetime earnings of $185,292.
b.   1990 Bonanza Champion.
c.   1990 NCHA Super Stakes NP Co-Res Champ.
d.   1992 Augusta Classic Non Pro Champion

17. DOC PEPPY GEM
a.   lifetime earnings of $182,056.20.
b.   1988 Non Pro Futurity finalist.
c.   1990 Super Stakes Open finalist.
d   990 NCHA Super Stakes Non-Pro Champion.
e.   Big D PCCHA Classic Champion.

18. PEPTOBOONSMAL
a.   lifetime earnings of $180,487.
b.   1995 NCHA Futurity Champion.
c.   Gold Coast Winter Champion.
d.   Bonanza Cutting Champion.
e.   1996 NCHA Derby finalist.
f.   1996 NCHA Super Stakes finalist.

19. BRIGAPEP
a.   lifetime earnings of $169,838.
b.   NCHA Non-Pro Futurity Champion.

20. POP A TOP PEP
a.   lifetime earnings of $162,593.
b.   1989 - 3rd NCHA Futurity.
c.   Augusta Futurity Champion.
d.   6th in 1990 Bonanza.
e.   Southern Cutting Futurity finalist.

21. POCO SAN SCORPION
a.   lifetime earnings of $146,460.95.
b.   1989 NCHA Futurity, Co Reserve Champion.
c.   NCHA Super Stakes Classic/Chall. Champ.

22. PEPPYS FROM HEAVEN
a.   lifetime earnings of $141,573.
b.   1990 NCHA Futurity; 6th Open, 14th NP.
c.   1991 NCHA Derby Non Pro Champion

23. PEPPY SHEA
a.   lifetime earnings of $137,585..
b.   1985 Tropicana Spectacular Res Champ.
c.   TQHA National Stakes Reserve Champion.
d.   1985 Big D PCHA Derby Champion.

24. POWDER RIVER PLAYBOY
a.   lifetime earnings of $137,114.
b.   1986 NCHA Futurity - 5th.
c.   1987 Bonanza Champion.

25. CALS SAN BADGER
a.   lifetime earnings of $135,128.
b.   1986 NCHA Futurity Co-Reserve Champion.

Photo by Janell Kleberg

A King Ranch branding iron.

The "Little Peppy" brand.

Photo by Janell Kleberg

Buster Welch with Little Peppy.

Buster cutting on Little Peppy at the Norias Division of King Ranch.

Photo by Janell Kleberg

*Peppy San Badger
"Little Peppy"*

Photo by Hal Hawkins

*Steve Knudsen, Little Peppy, Chris Kleberg
and Thomas Espy.*

Little Peppy, September 1996 being led by Dr. John Toelkes.

Little Peppy in front of his name marker at King Ranch.